MEASUREMENT 3/4

Walker Maths Essentials: Measurement 3/4
1st Edition
Charlotte Walker
Victoria Walker

Designer: Cheryl Smith, Macarn Design
Production controller: Magda Koralewska

Any URLs contained in this publication were checked for currency during the production process. Note, however, that the publisher cannot vouch for the ongoing currency of URLs.

Acknowledgements
Cover photo courtesy of Shutterstock.

We wish to thank the Boards of Trustees of Darfield and Riccarton High Schools for allowing us to use materials and ideas developed while teaching. Our thanks also go to all past and present colleagues, especially Kath Wilson, who have generously shared their experience and ideas.

For product information and technology assistance,
in Australia call **1300 790 853**;
in New Zealand call **0800 449 725**

For permission to use material from this text or product, please email **aust.permissions@cengage.com**

National Library of New Zealand Cataloguing-in-Publication Data
A catalogue record for this book is available from the National Library of New Zealand.

978 0 17 044717 1

Cengage Learning Australia
Level 7, 80 Dorcas Street
South Melbourne, Victoria Australia 3205

For learning solutions, visit **cengage.co.nz**

Printed in China by 1010 Printing International Limited.
4 5 6 7 25

Throughout this book:
Assume that diagrams are not drawn to scale.

CONTENTS

Glossary

Make your own glossary of key terms:

Term	Definition	Picture/Example
Units		
Perimeter		
Area		
Volume		
Capacity		
Polygon		
Compound shape		
Regular shape		
Cube		

 ISBN: 9780170447171

Cuboid		
Weight vs Mass		
Kilo		
Centi		
Milli		
Digital time		
Analogue time		
12-hour time		
24-hour time		

ISBN: 9780170447171

The language of measurement

Volume and capacity

- **Volume** measures how much **space** is taken up by an object.
  Units: mm^3, cm^3, m^3.
- **Capacity** measures the **amount that an object can hold**.
  Units: mL, L.
- Sometimes these terms are used interchangeably.

Example: Consider a thermos flask.
Its volume is the amount of space taken up by the thermos flask.
Its capacity is the amount of liquid that it can hold.

Match these words to measurement ideas below.

early	steep	full	short	warm
slope	late	heat	flat	day
hot	heavy	distance	fever	decline
long	empty	cold	week	light

Length ____________________

____

____

____

Angle ____________________

____

____

____

Time ____________________

____

____

____

Temperature ____________________

____

____

____

____

Volume/Capacity ____________________

____

Mass ____________________

____

ISBN: 9780170447171

Useful terms

Match the expressions on the left with their meaning or measure on the right.

1	A dozen	•	•	100
2	A generation	•	•	About 12
3	Days in September	•	•	366
4	Seasons in a year	•	•	365
5	Days in a year	•	•	10
6	Annual	•	•	Once a year
7	Years in a decade	•	•	31
8	Weeks in a month	•	•	Two weeks
9	A baker's dozen	•	•	30
10	Months in a year	•	•	About 52
11	Length of a fortnight	•	•	13
12	Days in a leap year	•	•	About four
13	Days in January	•	•	12
14	Weeks in spring	•	•	About 25 years
15	Years in a century	•	•	Four
16	Weeks in a year	•	•	12

ISBN: 9780170447171

Measuring devices

Match these measuring devices to what they would be used to measure.

ruler	pedometer	cup	timer
protractor	measuring cup	magnetic compass	tape measure
tablespoon	syringe	clock	scales
stopwatch	teaspoon	thermometer	odometer

Length ______________________

____

____

____

Capacity ______________________

____

____

____

____

Mass ______________________

Time ______________________

____

____

Angle ______________________

____

Temperature ______________________

Use some of the terms from the box above to label these instruments:

1 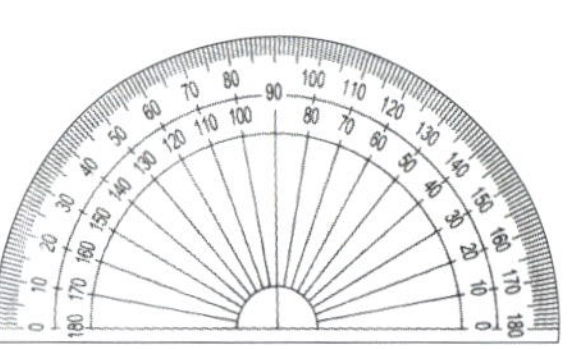

____

2 

____

3 

____

4 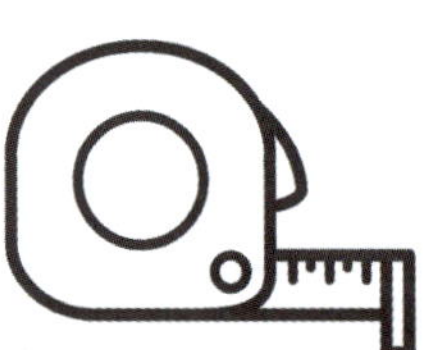

____

5 

____

6 

____

 ISBN: 9780170447171

Units

Abbreviations (shortened versions) for units

s	cm	m	tsp	c	L
kg	km	min	h	mg	t
mm	g	d	°C	mL	tbsp

Write the shortened version of these terms from the box above and identify what they are used to measure.

Unit of measurement	Shortened version
Kilogram	
Centimetre	cm
Metre	
Minute	
Litre	
Hectare	
Milligram	
Teaspoon	
Day	

Unit of measurement	Shortened version
Kilometre	
Millimetre	
Degree Celsius	
Second	
Tablespoon	
Tonne	
Millilitre	
Cup	
Gram	

Add each of these abbreviations to the boxes below.

Length	Mass
Capacity	Time
Temperature	

ISBN: 9780170447171

Time

- Time can be measured in **seconds**, **hours**, **days**, etc.

Use the following chart to help you convert time.

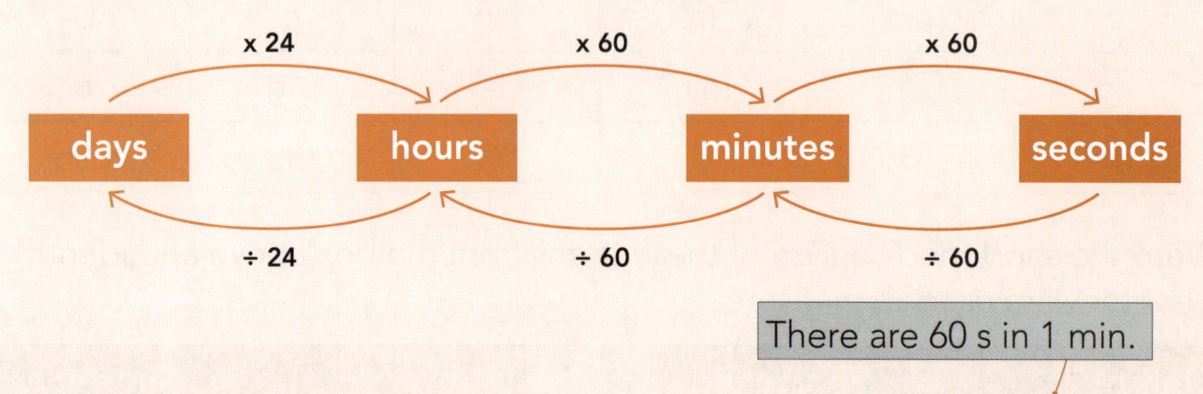

There are 60 s in 1 min.

Example: How many seconds are in 9 minutes?

9 min = 9 x 60
= 540 s

Highlight the correct conversion for each of the following.

1	2 hours	160 min	1 d
		120 min	60 min
3	2 days	24 h	72 h
		600 s	48 h
5	1 day	42 h	1044 min
		1440 min	1404 min

2	4 minutes	120 s	240 s
		0.4 h	60 s
4	120 seconds	2 min	2 h
		0.2 min	3 min
6	90 minutes	6000 s	4500 s
		1.5 h	2 h

Convert the following.

7 300 s = ______________ min

8 3 d = ______________ h

9 600 min = ______________ h

10 4 h = ______________ min

ISBN: 9780170447171

Highlight the longer period of time.

11	3 h	200 min	**12**	5 d	150 h
13	2 min	100 s	**14**	350 min	6 h
15	12 d	300 h	**16**	2 h	120 s
17	97 hours	4 d	**18**	1 d	1441 s

Put these times in order from shortest to longest. Hint: Rewrite them using the same units.

19

1450 min	1 d	93 600 s	25 h

Shortest Longest

Circle or highlight the most appropriate unit of time for these intervals.

20 The time it takes to boil a jug.

days hours minutes seconds

21 The time it takes to turn the light off.

days hours minutes seconds

22 The time it takes to grow a plant.

days hours minutes seconds

23 The amount of time you slept last night.

days hours minutes seconds

24 The time it takes to butter a piece of toast.

days hours minutes seconds

25 The time it takes to fly from Auckland to Dunedin.

days hours minutes seconds

ISBN: 9780170447171

Length

- The basic unit for measuring length is the **metre**.
- All other units of length in the metric system are based on the metre.

Use the following chart to help you convert lengths.

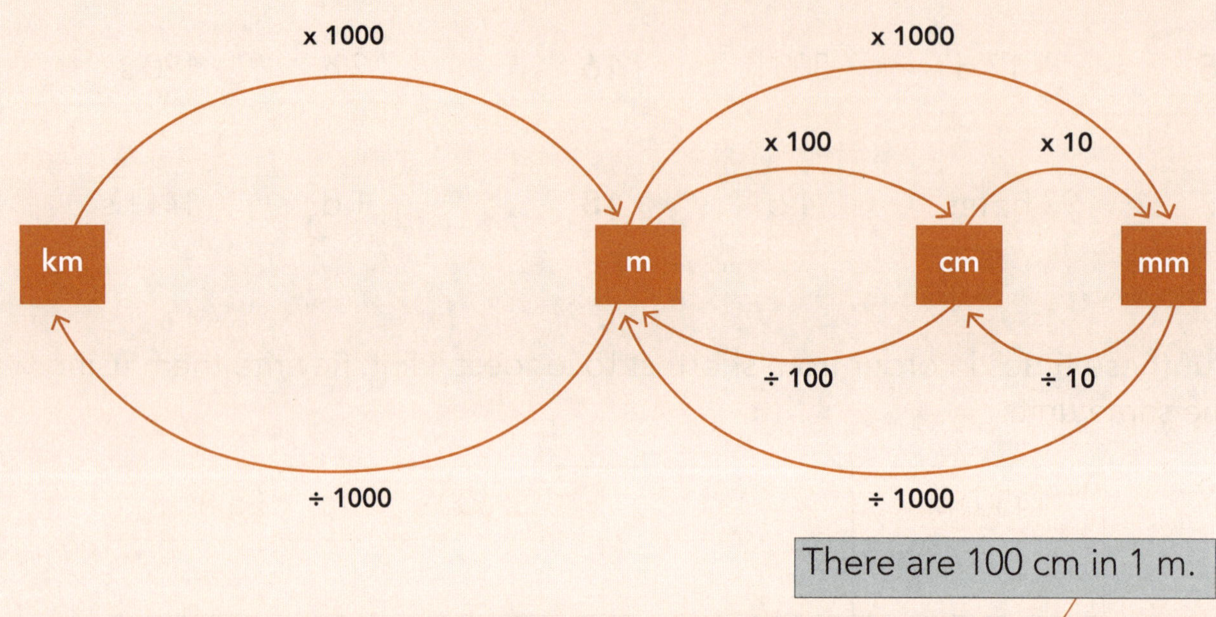

There are 100 cm in 1 m.

Example: How many centimetres are in 4 metres? 4 m = 4 x 100
= 400 cm

Highlight the correct conversion for each of the following.

1	2 km	1000 m	2000 m
		20 000 m	200 m
3	5 m	50 000 cm	50 cm
		5000 cm	500 cm
5	80 000 m	8 km	800 km
		80 km	0.8 km

2	600 cm	0.6 m	0.06 m
		6 m	60 m
4	300 mm	0.03 cm	30 m
		0.3 cm	3 m
6	1 km	100 000 cm	10 000 cm
		1000 cm	1 000 000 cm

ISBN: 9780170447171

Convert the following.

7 7 cm = ____________ mm

8 6 m = ____________ cm

9 5000 m = ____________ km

10 1.5 km = ____________ m

11 2400 cm = ____________ m

12 85 cm = ____________ mm

Highlight the greater length.

13 10 cm 110 mm

14 25 m 205 cm

15 50 m 5 km

16 450 mm 54 cm

17 301 cm 3 m

18 900 mm 9 cm

Put these lengths in order from shortest to longest. Hint: Rewrite them using the same units.

19

100 m	1 km	100 cm	10 000 mm

Shortest Longest

20

0.5 km	5500 mm	55 m	500 cm

Shortest Longest

ISBN: 9780170447171

Circle or highlight the most likely unit of measurement for these items.

21 The height of your desk.

km m cm mm

22 The thickness of your bank card.

km m cm mm

23 The length of a pen.

km m cm mm

24 The distance from Christchurch to Nelson.

km m cm mm

25 The length of your foot.

km m cm mm

26 The length of your classroom.

km m cm mm

27 The length of a spider.

km m cm mm

28 The length of the cross-country.

km m cm mm

Estimating length

From the list on the right, select the most likely for the following. You may need to do some research.

29 The height of a basketball hoop: ____________

30 The height of a giraffe: ____________

31 The height of a drink bottle: ____________

32 The distance between Auckland and Hamilton: ____________

33 The thickness of a cellphone: ____________

34 The length of a bumblebee: ____________

35 The length of a hockey stick: ____________

9 mm
21 cm
6 m
124 km
76 cm
305 cm
1.4 cm

 ISBN: 9780170447171

Mass

- The basic unit for measuring mass is the **gram**.
- All other units of mass in the metric system are based on the gram.
- Mass is often mistakenly called weight.

Weight is a measure of the pull of gravity on an object and is measured in **newtons**.

Mass is the amount of matter an object contains and is measured in **grams**.

Use the following chart to help you convert mass.

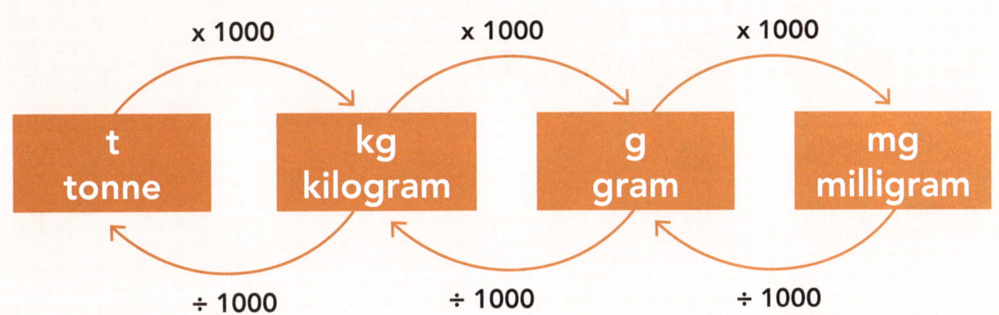

There are 1000 g in 1 kg.

Example: How many grams are in 4 kilograms?

4 kg = 4 x 1000
= 4000 g

Highlight the correct conversion for each of the following.

1	3 g	300 mg	3000 mg
		30 mg	30 000 mg
3	4000 mg	40 g	4 g
		0.4 g	400 g
5	80 g	800 000 kg	8000 mg
		80 000 mg	800 mg

2	2 kg	200 g	200 000 g
		20 000 g	2000 g
4	5 t	50 kg	50 000 kg
		500 kg	5000 kg
6	10 000 kg	10 t	1000 t
		100 t	1 t

ISBN: 9780170447171

Convert the following.

7 12 kg = __________ g

8 3 t = __________ kg

9 5000 mg = __________ g

10 6500 g = __________ kg

11 15 g = __________ mg

12 20 000 kg = __________ t

Highlight the greater mass.

13 9 g 9001 mg

14 4 kg 400 g

15 3000 mg 30 g

16 2 t 20 000 kg

17 500 kg 5 t

18 100 000 mg 1 kg

Put these masses in order from smallest to largest. Hint: Rewrite them using the same units.

19

100 000 g	10 kg	1 t	10 000 mg

Smallest Largest

20

99 kg	0.1 t	900 g	9 000 000 mg

Smallest Largest

ISBN: 9780170447171

Circle or highlight the most likely unit of measurement for these items.

21 The mass of a bus.

t kg g mg

22 The mass of a school bag.

t kg g mg

23 The mass of a feijoa.

t kg g mg

24 The mass of a mosquito.

t kg g mg

25 The mass of a $1 coin.

t kg g mg

26 The mass of a box of cereal.

t kg g mg

27 The mass of a toddler.

t kg g mg

28 The mass of desk.

t kg g mg

Estimating mass

From the list on the right, select the most likely masses for the following. You may need to do some research.

29 The mass of a polar bear: ____________

30 The mass of a digger: ____________

31 The mass of a cellphone: ____________

32 The mass of a 10 cent coin: ____________

33 The mass of a feather: ____________

34 The mass of a bag of rice: ____________

35 The mass of a fridge: ____________

100 kg
1 kg
1 mg
1.5 t
450 kg
113 g
3.31 g

ISBN: 9780170447171

Capacity

- The basic unit for measuring capacity is the **litre**.
- All other units of capacity in the metric system are based on the litre.

Use the following chart to help you convert capacity.

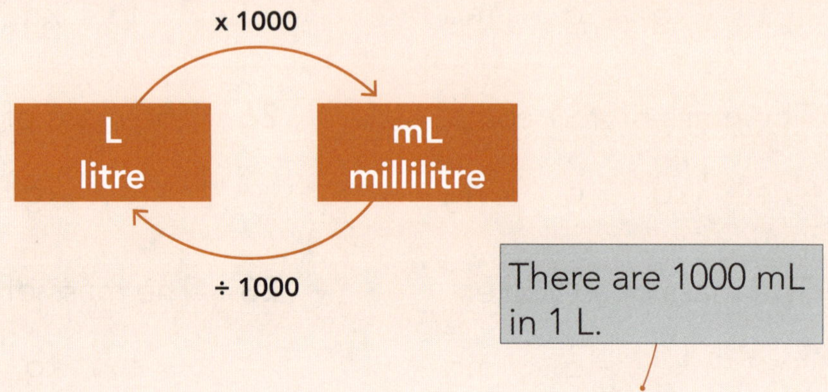

Example: How many millilitres are in 6 litres? 6 L = 6 x 1000
= 6000 mL

Highlight the correct conversion for each of the following.

1	1 L	100 mL	1000 mL	**2**	4000 mL	40 L	400 L
		10 mL	10 000 mL			4 L	4000 L
3	65 000 mL	65 L	650 L	**4**	2.5 L	25 mL	2500 mL
		6.5 L	6500 L			250 mL	5200 mL

Convert the following.

5 9 L = ______________ mL

6 6000 mL = ______________ L

7 11 000 mL = ______________ L

8 1.5 L = ______________ mL

9 24 L = ______________ mL

10 75 000 mL = ______________ L

ISBN: 9780170447171

Put these capacities in order from smallest to largest. Hint: Rewrite them using the same units.

11

1100 mL	1 L	1001 mL	1010 mL	10 L

Smallest Largest

12

1.5 L	1050 mL	5 L	5001 mL	1000 mL

Smallest Largest

Estimating capacity

From the list on the right, select the most likely capacities for the following. You may need to do some research.

13 The capacity of a spa pool: ____________

14 The capacity of a small can of drink: ____________

15 The capacity of a teaspoon: ____________

16 The capacity of a bottle of shampoo: ____________

17 The capacity of a backpack: ____________

18 The capacity of a watering can: ____________

26 L
700 mL
1000 L
5 mL
8 L
250 mL

ISBN: 9780170447171

Appropriate units

- Length is measured in mm, cm, m or km.
- Mass is measured in mg, g, kg or t.
- Capacity is measured in mL or L.
- Time is measured in seconds, minutes, hours or days.

Example: The mass of this car would be measured in which of the following units?

cm **g** **t** **L**

The most appropriate answer is t (tonnes).

Circle or highlight the most appropriate unit of measurement for these items.

1 The length of a running race.

km mL mm g

2 The amount of liquid in a cup of tea.

kg L cm mL

3 The mass of a rat.

cm kg L g

4 The length of a television show.

min L cm s

5 The length of a mobile phone.

mL km min cm

6 The amount of sauce in a bottle.

mg mL days g

7 The mass of a whale.

L g s t

8 The width of your calculator.

km kg L cm

9 The amount of water used in a shower.

mL t L kg

10 The length of time it takes to wash your hands.

d mL cm s

11 The length of a T-shirt.

mL g cm min

12 The mass of a toddler.

cm kg mm mg

ISBN: 9780170447171

Estimating quantities

Use the most appropriate quantities from the right column to complete the following sentences. You may need to do some research.

A

1	The height of Mt Taranaki is most likely to be ________.	15 mm
2	The length of the Queen Charlotte tramping track is most likely to be ________.	30.5 m
3	The length of your big toe nail is most likely to be ________.	2518 m
4	The length of a carrot is most likely to be ________.	70 mm
5	The length of a netball court is most likely to be ________.	1.5 m
6	The length of your intestines is most likely to be ________.	1600 km
7	The length of New Zealand is most likely to be ________.	72 km
8	The length of a frog is most likely to be ________.	18 cm

B

1	The mass of a crocodile is most likely to be ________.	18 t
2	The capacity of your kitchen sink is most likely to be ________.	5 kg
3	The mass of a can of baked beans is most likely to be ________.	20 L
4	The mass of your calculator is most likely to be ________.	550 kg
5	The mass of a fly is most likely to be ________.	420 g
6	The capacity of a tablespoon is most likely to be ________.	1 500 000 L
7	The mass of a bowling ball most likely to be ________.	0.01 g
8	The capacity of a school swimming pool is most likely to be ________.	2.7 g
9	The mass of a table tennis ball is most likely to be ________.	191 g
10	The mass of a full cement truck is most likely to be ________.	14.8 mL

ISBN: 9780170447171

Conversion cross-number

Fill in the white squares in this cross-number with a digit. Some decimal points (•) have been put in for you.

1	2			3	4	5		6	7 •	8
9			10			•			11	
12	•			13	•			14		
15			16	•			17		18	
		19	•			20	•	21		
	22						23			
24		25		26		27				28
29	30		31	•	32				33	
34	•			35				36		
37			38		•				39	
40				41				42	•	

 ISBN: 9780170447171

ACROSS

1 15.0 cm to mm
3 0.320 km to m
6 0.0017 kg to g
9 Days in April
10 8000 mm to cm
11 Number in a dozen
12 500 g to kg
13 8 mm to cm
14 450 000 mL to L
15 A baker's dozen
16 6000 kg to t
18 Years in a decade
19 9000 mL to L
20 3 mm to cm
22 Days in twenty weeks
23 Days in a leap year
25 Seconds in twelve minutes
27 g in 0.160 kg
29 Weeks in a year
31 500 kg to t
33 Days in August
34 600 cm to m
35 Days in a year
36 Days in sixteen fortnights
37 40 000 g to kg
38 Months in four years
39 Days in fourteen weeks
40 Years in a century
41 A dozen dozens
42 Litres in 7000 mL

DOWN

1 13.010 m to mm
2 50 300 mL to L
3 0.3 km to m
4 200 mm to cm
5 800 g to kg
7 151 m to km
8 72 kg to g
16 6020 kg to t
17 360 mg to g
19 94.7 cm to mm
21 Minutes in six hours
24 75 601 000 mL to L
26 381 mg to g
27 10.504 t to kg
28 91.480 kg to g
30 2400 mm to m
32 56 400 kg to t
33 329 000 m to km

ISBN: 9780170447171

Word questions

1 Juliet's oranges weighed 900 g. If she had five oranges, how much does each weigh?

2 Beau needs 180 g of flour per cake. If he wants to make three cakes, how much flour will he need?

3 Theo has 5 m of tape and uses 140 cm. How much tape does he have left?

4 A bee can fly 21 km each hour. How far could it travel in 20 minutes?

5 It's recommended that you should wash your hands for 20 seconds. If you wash your hands three times a day, how long have you spent washing your hands in a week?

6 Guinea pigs need 18 g of pellets per day. If you have two guinea pigs, how much will they eat in a month (30 days)?

7 **a** Jeremiah runs 5.6 km per day. How far will he have run in a year if he runs every day?

b He gets an injury, which means he can't train for the last seven weeks of the year. How far had he run before he was injured?

 ISBN: 9780170447171

Time

Digital and analogue time

1 Digital time

Start of the day is at 12.00 a.m.
End of the morning is at 11.59 a.m.
Start of the afternoon is at 12.00 p.m.
End of the day is at 11.59 p.m.

2 Analogue time

This is the time shown on a clock face.

3 Time with words

Quarter to three.
Half past four.

Examples:

Digital time	Analogue time	Time with words
12.05	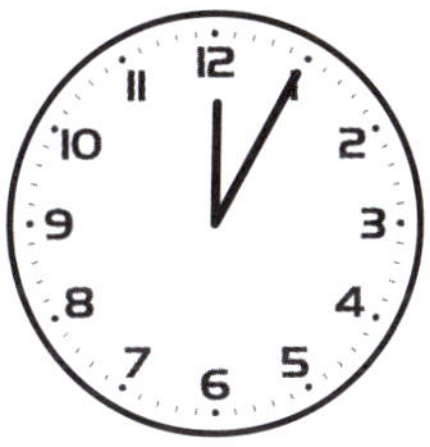	Five past twelve

Highlight the correct conversion for each of the following.

1	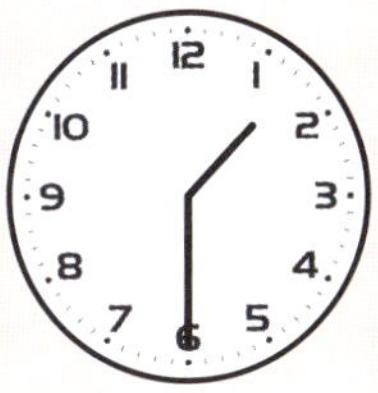	2.30	1.30
		6.07	1.20
2	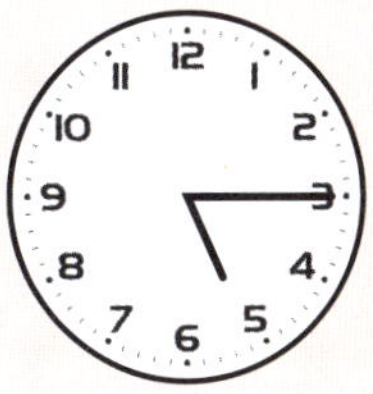	3.26	3.25
		5.10	5.15
3	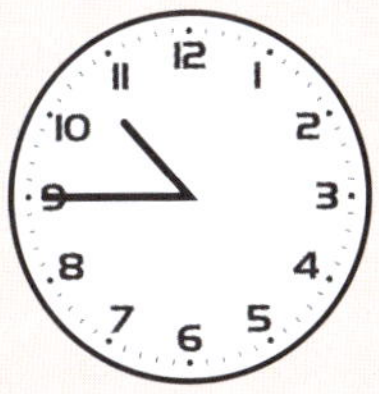	11.45	9.54
		10.45	10.40
4	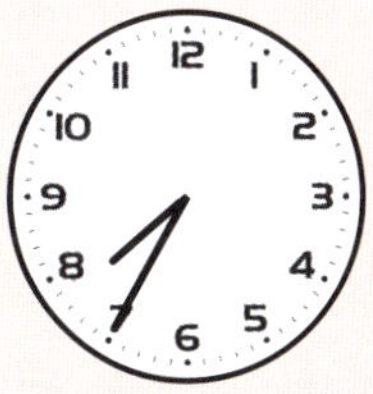	8.35	7.35
		7.37	8.37

Convert these analogue times to digital times.

5 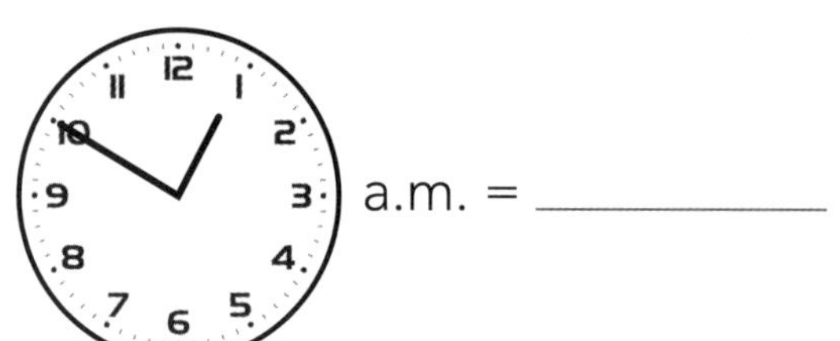 a.m. = ____________

6 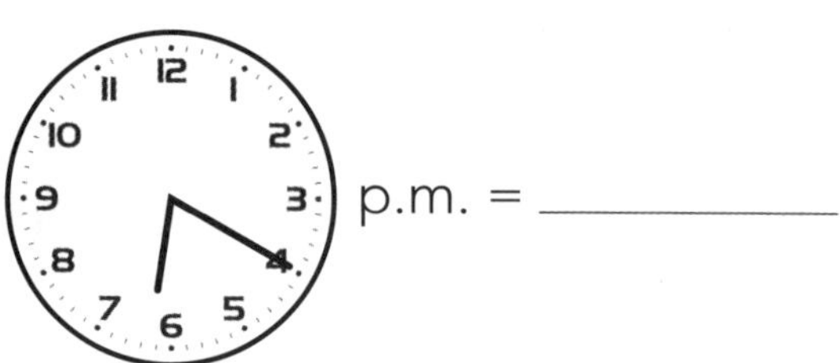 p.m. = ____________

7 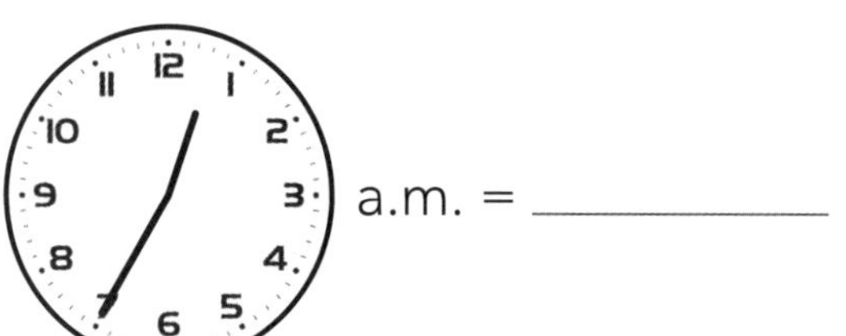 a.m. = ____________

8 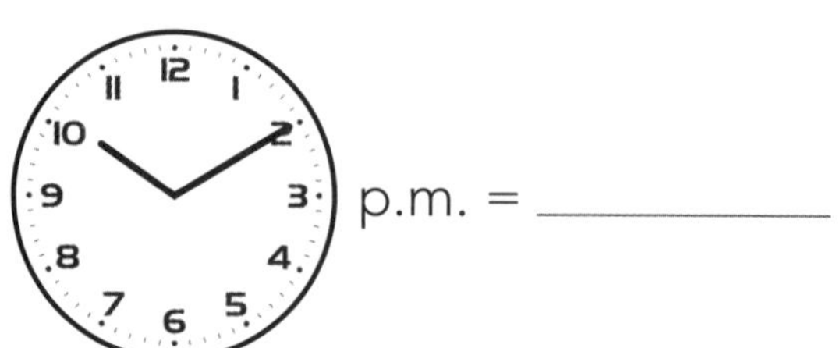 p.m. = ____________

9 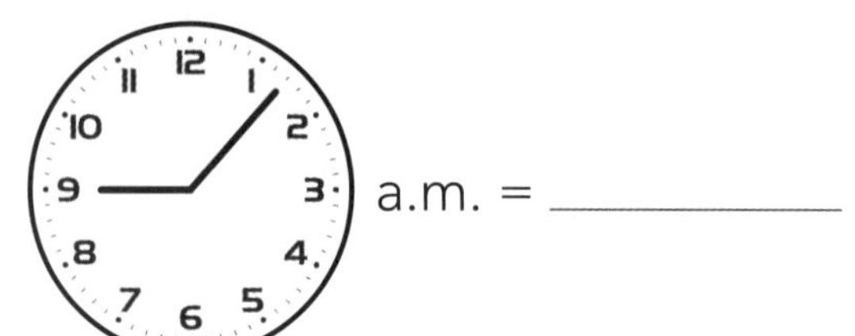 a.m. = ____________

10 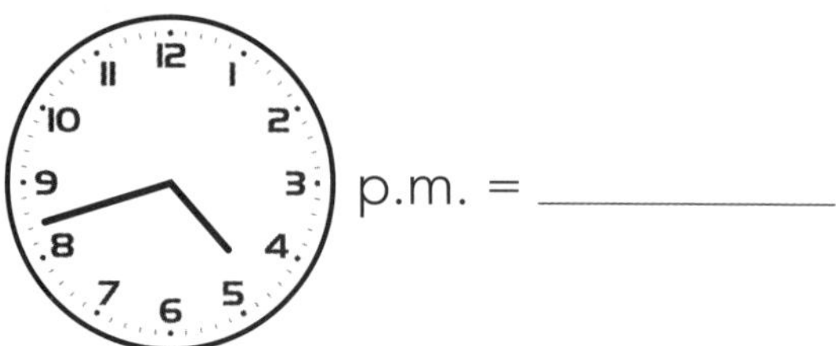 p.m. = ____________

Convert these statements to digital times.

11 Quarter to nine:

____________ a.m.

12 Five past four:

____________ a.m.

13 Twenty to five:

____________ a.m.

14 Twenty past eleven:

____________ p.m.

15 Quarter past two:

____________ a.m.

16 Half past one:

____________ p.m.

17 Ten to eleven:

____________ p.m.

18 Noon:

____________ p.m.

19 Midday:

____________ p.m.

20 Midnight:

____________ a.m.

ISBN: 9780170447171

Convert these analogue times to words.

21 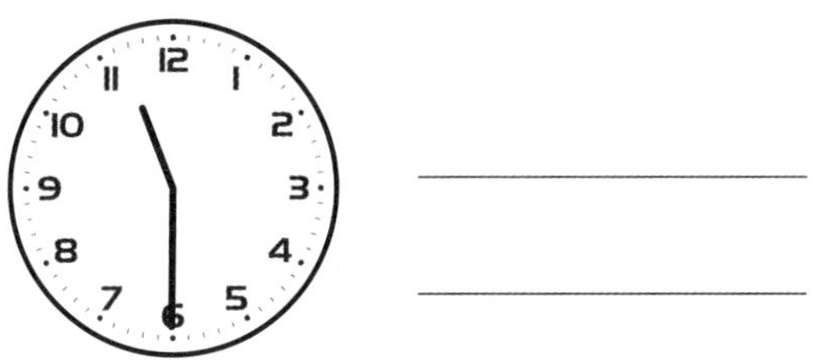

22 

23 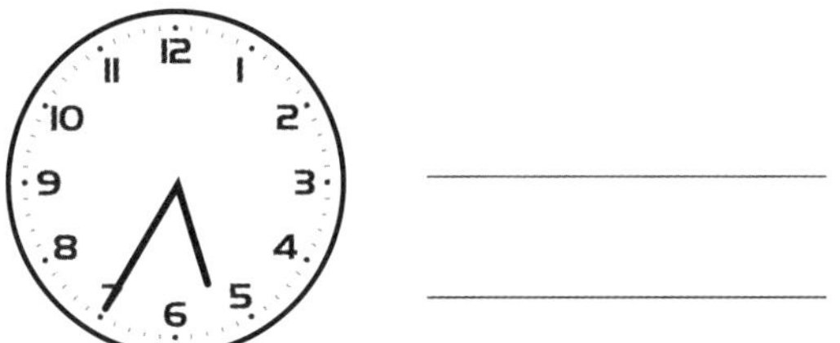

24 

25 

26 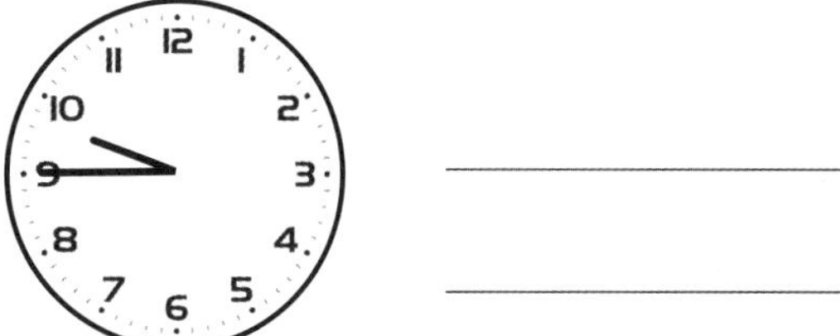

Write a digital time that is half an hour after these times.

27 Quarter to ten:

_____________ p.m.

28 3.50 p.m.:

_____________ p.m.

29 9.12 a.m.:

_____________ a.m.

30 Five to one:

_____________ p.m.

Write a digital time that is 15 minutes before these times.

31 Twenty past two:

_____________ a.m.

32 9.40 p.m.:

_____________ p.m.

33 Five past ten:

_____________ p.m.

34 1.13 p.m.:

_____________ p.m.

ISBN: 9780170447171

Connect the dots

Digital time	Analogue time	Time with words
2.45 •	•  •	• Twenty to three
4.15 •	•  •	• Quarter to three
4.10 •	•  •	• Ten to five
5.25 •	•  •	• Half past four
4.50 •	•  •	• Quarter past four
2.40 •	•  •	• Ten past four
4.30 •	•  •	• Twenty-five past five

ISBN: 9780170447171

24-hour and 12-hour time

There are two ways of writing times:

12-hour time can also be written with a full stop, e.g. 1.00 a.m.

24-hour time can also be written without the colon, e.g. 0000.

12-hour time	24-hour time
Midnight	00:00
1:00 a.m.	01:00
2:00 a.m.	02:00
3:00 a.m.	03:00
4:00 a.m.	04:00
5:00 a.m.	05:00
6:00 a.m.	06:00
7:00 a.m.	07:00
8:00 a.m.	08:00
9:00 a.m.	09:00
10:00 a.m.	10:00
11:00 a.m.	11:00
Midday or noon	12:00
1:00 p.m.	13:00
2:00 p.m.	14:00
3:00 p.m.	15:00
4:00 p.m.	16:00
5:00 p.m.	17:00
6:00 p.m.	18:00
7:00 p.m.	19:00
8:00 p.m.	20:00
9:00 p.m.	21:00
10:00 p.m.	22:00
11:00 p.m.	23:00

Midnight or 12:00 a.m.

a.m. tells you that a time is in the morning.

Midday or noon or 12:00 p.m.

p.m. tells you that a time is in the afternoon or evening.

24 hour time has **four digits**, so a **0** is added to the start of times earlier than 10 a.m.

Between 1 p.m. and 11:59 p.m: To convert 12-hour times into 24-hour time, you need to add 12 hours.

ISBN: 9780170447171

Examples:

		12-hour time	24-hour time
1	Five minutes past midnight.	12:05 a.m.	00:05
2	One minute before midday.	11:59 a.m.	11:59
3	Ten minutes past midday.	12:10 p.m.	12:10
4	Two minutes before midnight.	11:58 p.m.	23:58

Highlight the correct conversion for each of the following.

1	6.43 p.m.	06:43	16:43
		18:34	18:43
3	22:19	22.19 p.m.	10.19 a.m.
		10.19 p.m.	11.19 p.m.
5	17:38	7.38 a.m.	5.38 p.m.
		5.38 a.m.	7.38 p.m.

2	5.21 a.m.	17:21	05:21
		05:12	15:21
4	9.56 p.m.	21:65	19:56
		09:56	21:56
6	8.12 a.m.	08:12	18:12
		16:12	16:21

Convert the following into 12-hour time.

7 07:39 = ____________

8 20:42 = ____________

9 15:06 = ____________

10 02:17 = ____________

11 22:01 = ____________

12 17:23 = ____________

13 09:56 = ____________

14 14:45 = ____________

ISBN: 9780170447171

Convert the following into 24-hour time.

15 6.17 a.m. = ____________

16 3.30 p.m. = ____________

17 8.43 p.m. = ____________

18 2.39 a.m. = ____________

19 11.10 p.m. = ____________

20 1.52 p.m. = ____________

21 p.m. = ____________

22 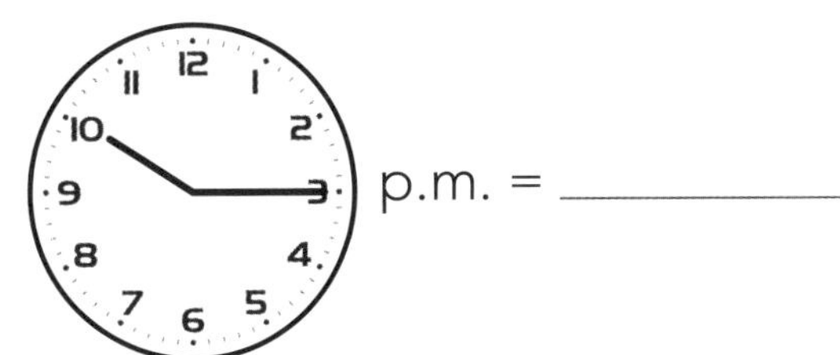 p.m. = ____________

23 a.m. = ____________

24 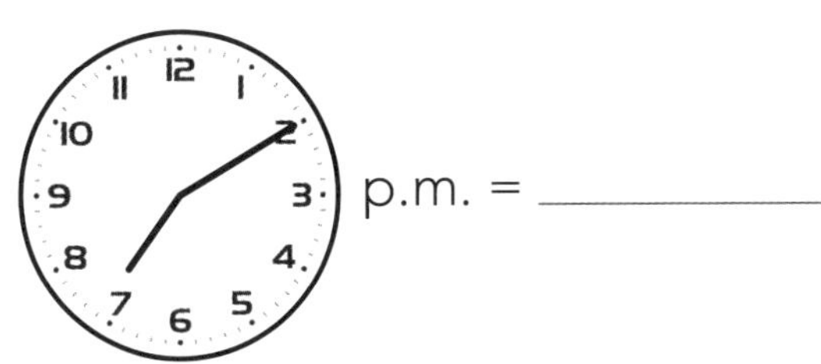 p.m. = ____________

25 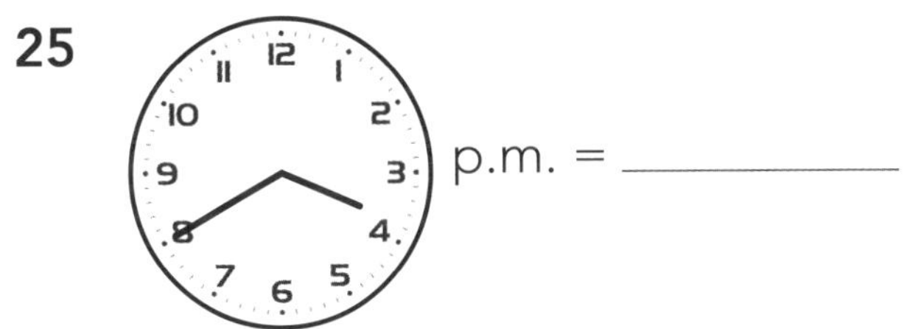 p.m. = ____________

26 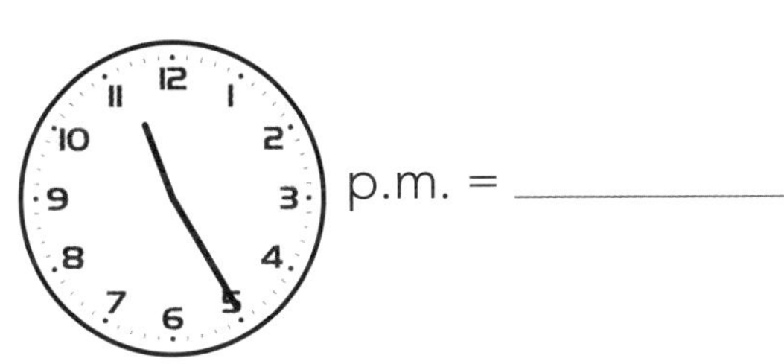 p.m. = ____________

27 Quarter to nine in the morning:

____

28 Five past four in the morning:

____

29 Twenty to five in the afternoon:

____

30 Twenty past eleven in the evening:

____

31 Quarter past two in the morning:

____

32 Half past one in the afternoon:

____

33 Ten to eleven at night:

____

34 Noon:

____

ISBN: 9780170447171

Highlight the time that is later in the day.

35	2.15 a.m.	02:51	**36**	6.59 p.m.	16:00
37	8.23 p.m.	18:32	**38**	07:25	7.20 a.m.
39	12:01 a.m.	12:10	**40**	20:00	2:00 p.m.

Put these times in order from earliest to latest in the day. Hint: Rewrite them using the same time format.

41

17:03	05:17	5.07 p.m.	7.05 a.m.	15:17

Earliest Latest

42

16:20	6.16 a.m.	18:20	06:18	6.18 p.m.

Earliest Latest

Complete the table.

		12-hour time	24-hour time
43	One minute past midday.		
44	Twenty-five minutes before midnight.		
45	Just before lunch at quarter to twelve.		
46	Five to one in the morning.		
47	One fifty-nine in the afternoon.		
48	Two minutes after midnight.		

ISBN: 9780170447171

Word questions

1 Lily's kitchen clock is reading 7 minutes fast. What time should she wind it back to?

____

2 It takes Tawhai 18 minutes to bike to rugby practice. What is the latest time he should leave if he needs to be there at 4.30 p.m.?

____

3 Tess puts a cake in the oven at 11.15 a.m. It needs 35 minutes to cook. When should she take it out?

____

4 A movie runs for 115 minutes. If it starts at 6.35 p.m., when does it finish?

____

5 A netball game starts at 9.55 a.m. and lasts for 40 minutes. At what time is half time?

____

6 A chess game starts at 10.47 a.m. and finishes at 11.23 a.m. How long did it take?

____

7 The ferry from Wellington to Picton takes 3 hours and 15 minutes. When will the 8.45 a.m. sailing dock in Picton?

____

8 An adventure race takes Kiri 8 hours and 36 minutes. If she started at 7.30 a.m., what time did she finish?

____

ISBN: 9780170447171

Reading tables

Answer the following questions.

Train timetable

City Centre	08:45	09:08	09:16	09:27
Miro Square	08:52	09:15	09:23	09:34
Kaka Pl	09:07	09:30	09:38	09:49
Tui St	09:16	09:39	09:47	09:58
River Rd	09:22	09:45	09:53	10:04
Lakeside	09:33	09:56	10:04	10:15

1 **a** If you take a train from City Centre to River Rd, how many stops do you pass?

____

b What time does the earliest train arrive at Lakeside?

____

c How long does the train take to get from Kaka Pl to Tui St?

____

d If Ari needs to be in Lakeside before 10 a.m., what train should he take from Miro Square?

____

Bus timetable

Rimu Ave	Kauri Lane	Kahikatea Way	Pohutukawa Rd
18:09	18:22	18:31	18:56
18:21	18:34	18:43	19:08
18:48	19:01	19:10	19:35
19:02	19:15	19:24	19:59
19:17	19:30	19:39	20:04
19:25	19:38	19:47	20:12
19:38	19:51	20:00	20:25

2 **a** What time does the 18:48 Rimu Ave bus arrive at Pohutukawa Rd?

____

b How long does it take to get from Kahikatea Way to Pohutukawa Rd?

____

c Joy needs to get from Rimu Ave to Kahikatea Way before 7.30 p.m. What bus should she take?

____

d Ralph arrives at Pohutukawa Rd just after 8 p.m. What bus did he take from Kauri Lane?

____

 ISBN: 9780170447171

Scales

Understanding scales

- Find **zero** on the scale to make sure that you read in the **correct direction**.
- If zero is not on the scale, make sure you read from **smaller values to larger values**.
- Include **units** in your answer.
- **Think** about your answer. Does it seem reasonable?

Here is how to work out the size of each gap between ticks on a scale.

Step 1: Calculate the **distance** between two **labelled** points.

Distance = 30 – 20 = **10 cm**

20 cm … 30

Step 2: Count the **number of gaps** between 20 and 30.
Number of gaps = 5.

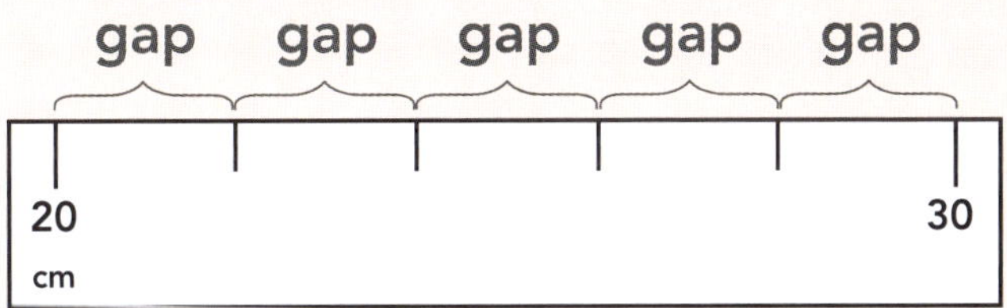

Step 3: Divide the distance by the number of gaps: $\frac{10}{5} = 2$ cm.

Step 4: Each gap along the number line is 2 on the scale.

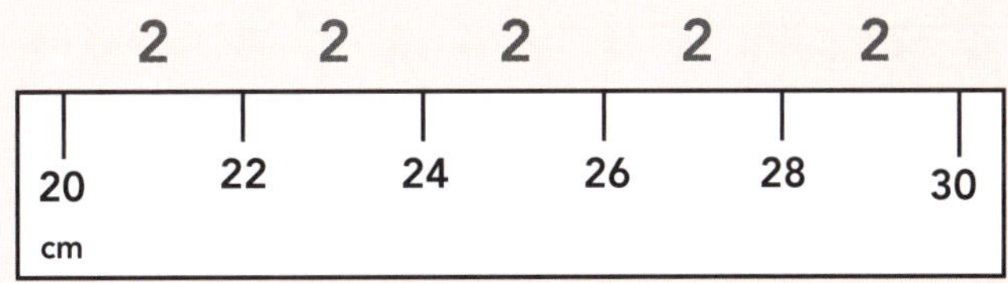

Calculate the sizes of the gaps and write the missing numbers on the scales.

1

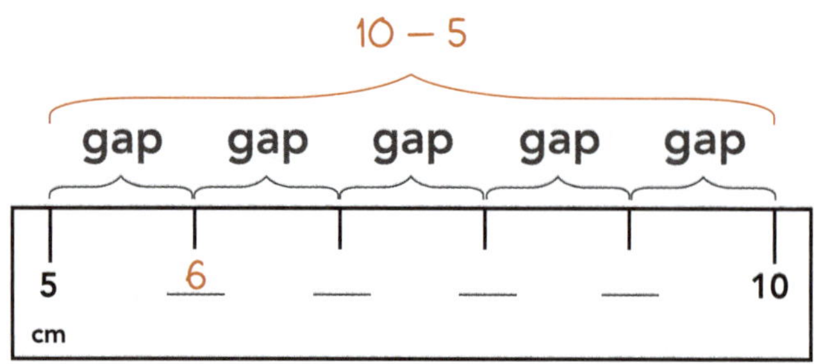

Size of gap = $\frac{\text{interval}}{\text{gaps}}$

= $\frac{10 - 5}{5}$

= 1

2

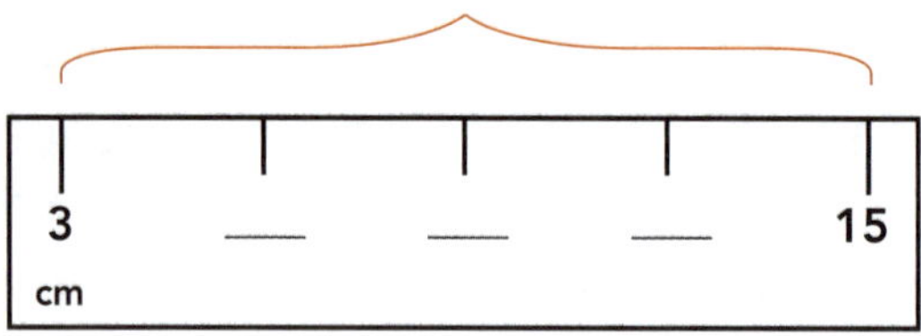

Size of gap = $\frac{\text{interval}}{\text{gaps}}$

= $\frac{\ -\ }{4}$

=

3

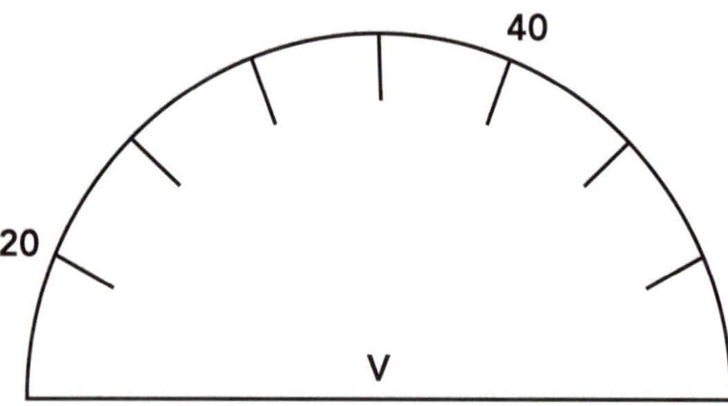

Size of gap = $\frac{\text{interval}}{\text{gaps}}$

=

=

4

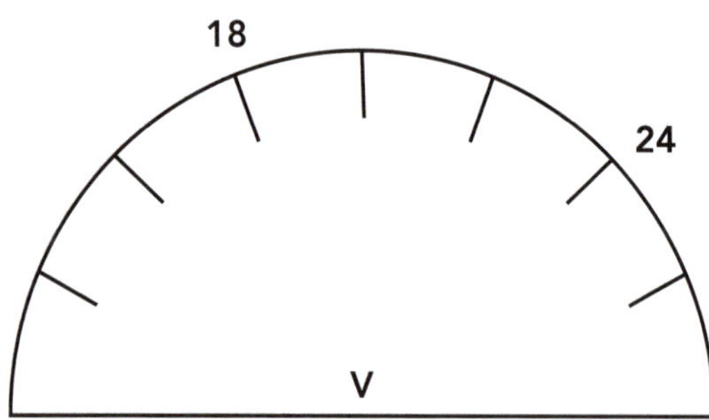

Size of gap =

5

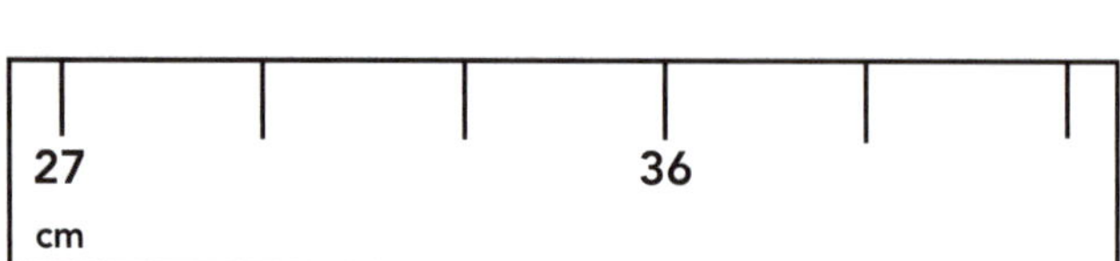

Size of gap =

 ISBN: 9780170447171

Reading scales

Write down the measurements shown on these scales.

1

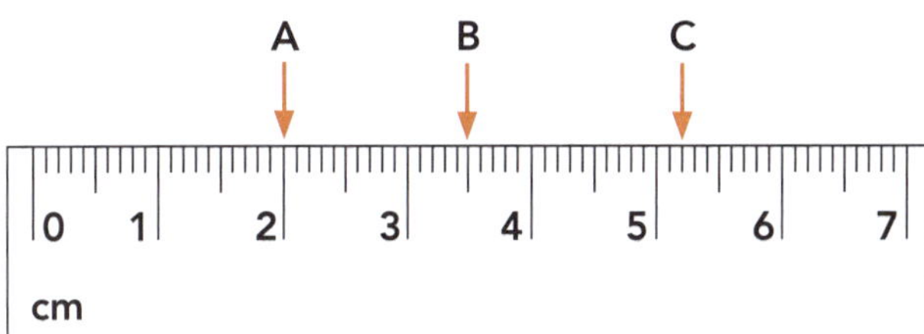

A = ____________

B = ____________

C = ____________

2

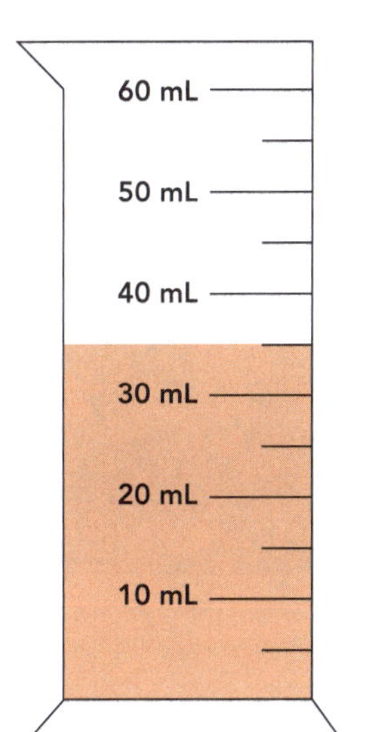

Volume = ____________

3

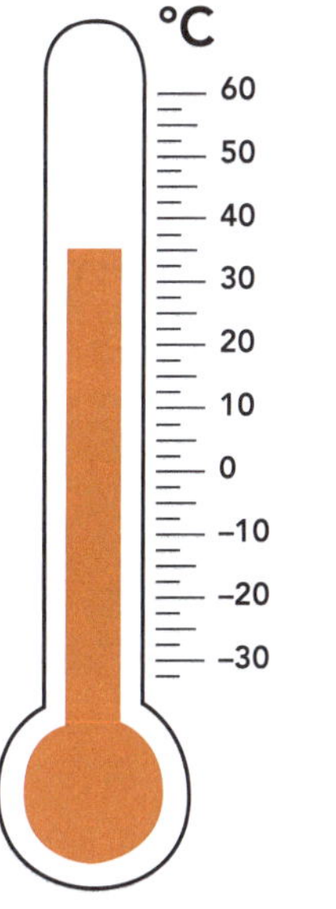

Temperature = ____________ °C

4

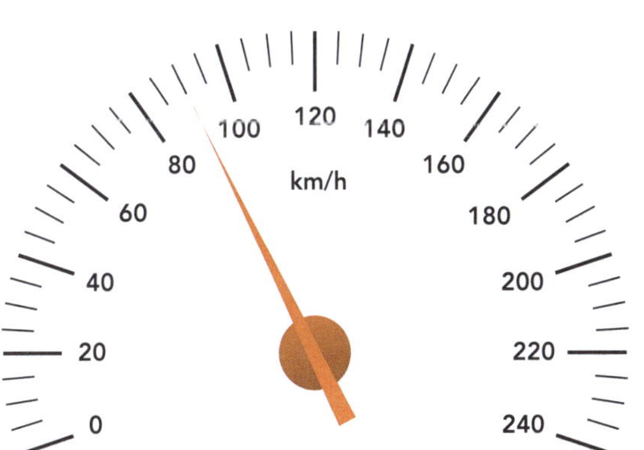

Speed = ____________ km/h

5

Mass = ____________ kg

ISBN: 9780170447171

6

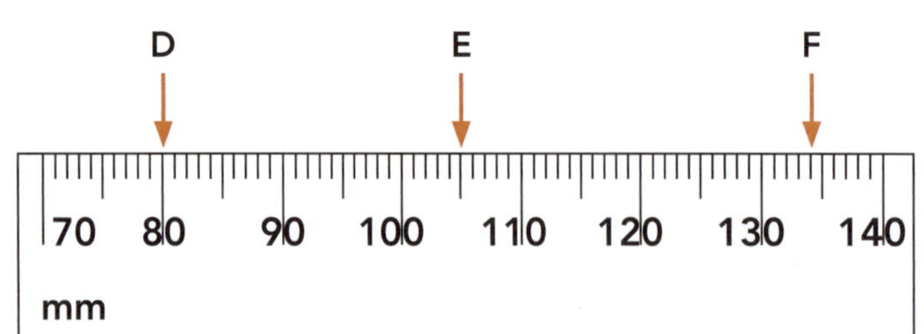

D = ________________

E = ________________

F = ________________

7

Voltage = ______________ V

8

Voltage = ______________ V

9

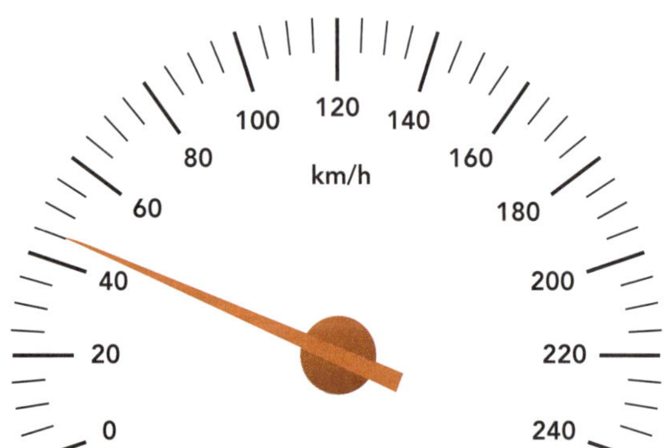

Speed = ______________ km/h

10

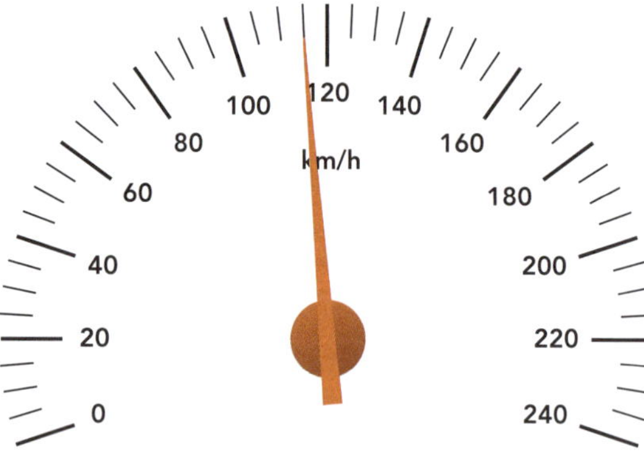

Speed = ______________ km/h

 ISBN: 9780170447171

Showing values on scales

Colour the diagrams or add an arrow to show these measurements.

1 25 mL

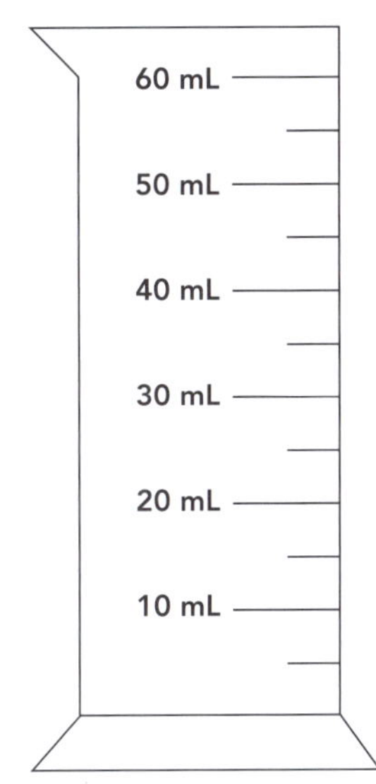

2 55 km/h

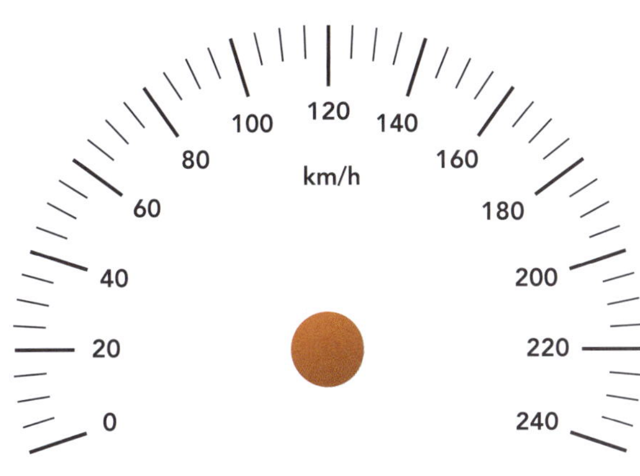

3

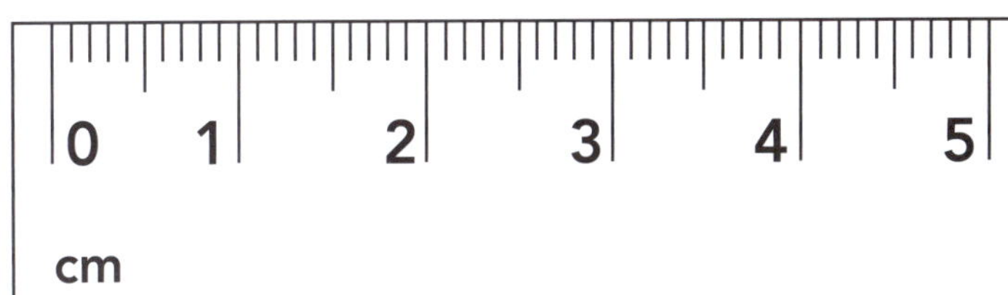

A = 4.3 cm

B = 2.4 cm

C = 0.9 cm

4 90 mL

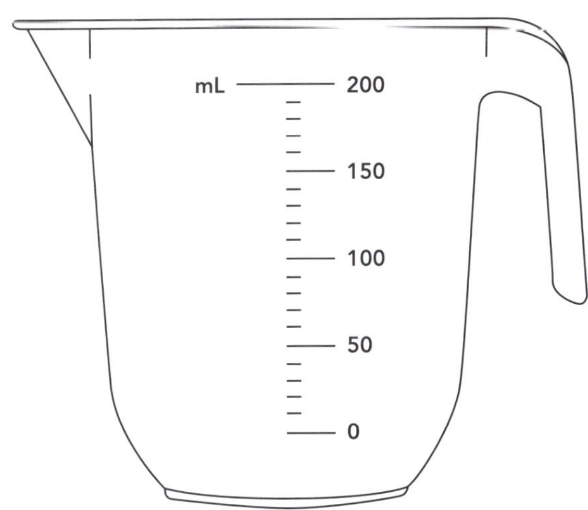

5 80°C

ISBN: 9780170447171

Perimeter

Shapes on a grid

- The perimeter is the **distance around the outside** of a two-dimensional (2D) shape.
- To find the perimeter, you need to **start at one corner** and **add** the distances around the outside of the shape.
- The shapes are drawn on a 1 cm by 1 cm grid.

Examples:

1 **2** It pays to use a dot to show where you started.

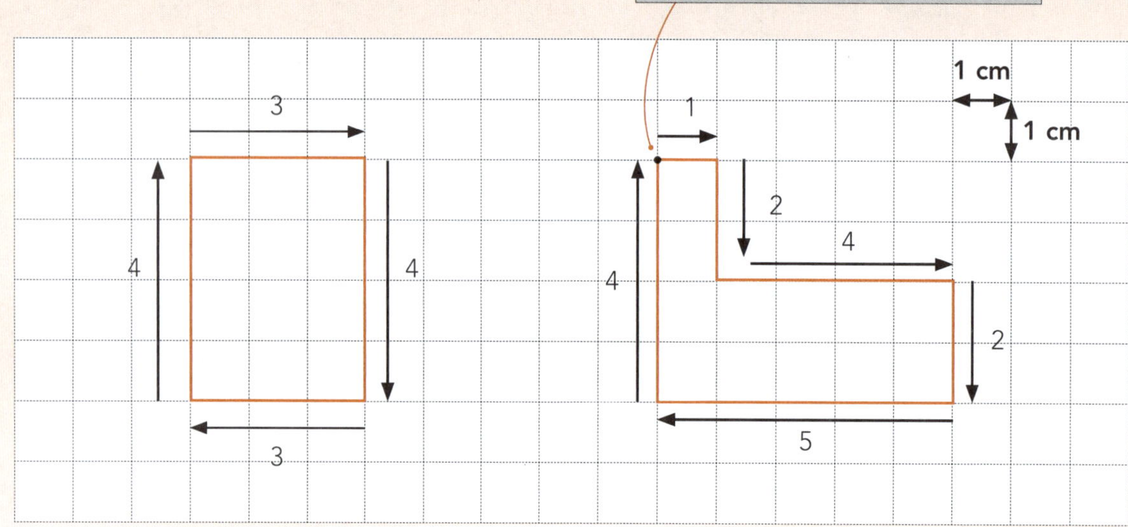

Perimeter = 4 + 3 + 4 + 3
= 14 cm

Perimeter = 1 + 2 + 4 + 2 + 5 + 4
= 18 cm

Calculate the perimeters of these shapes.

1

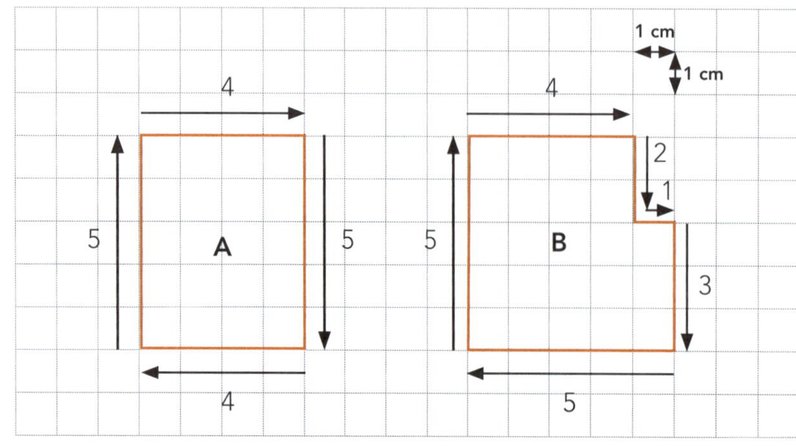

A = ______________

____

B = ______________

____

ISBN: 9780170447171

2

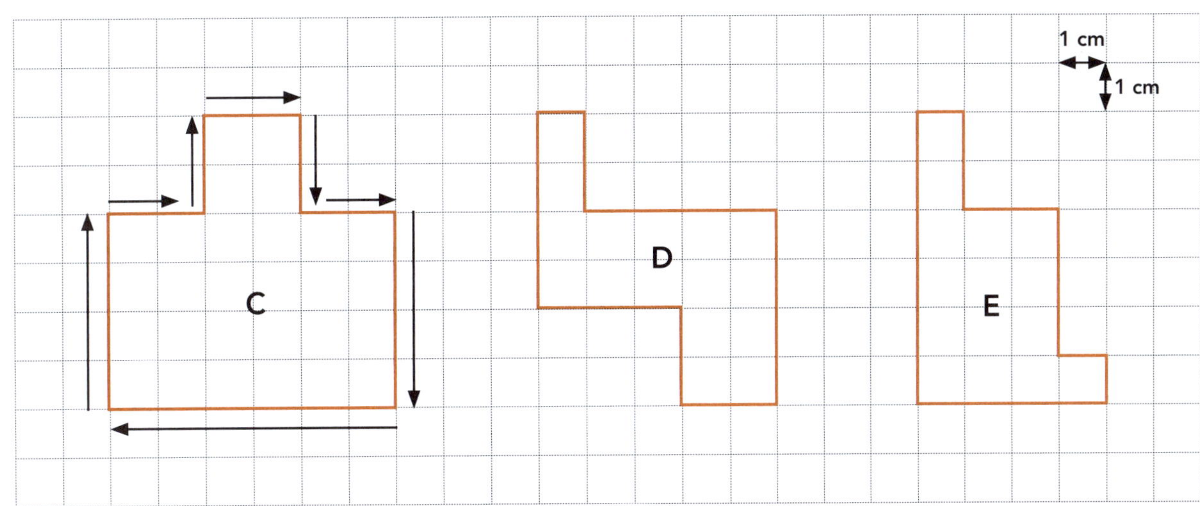

C = ______________________

____

____

D = ______________________

____

____

E = ______________________

____

____

3

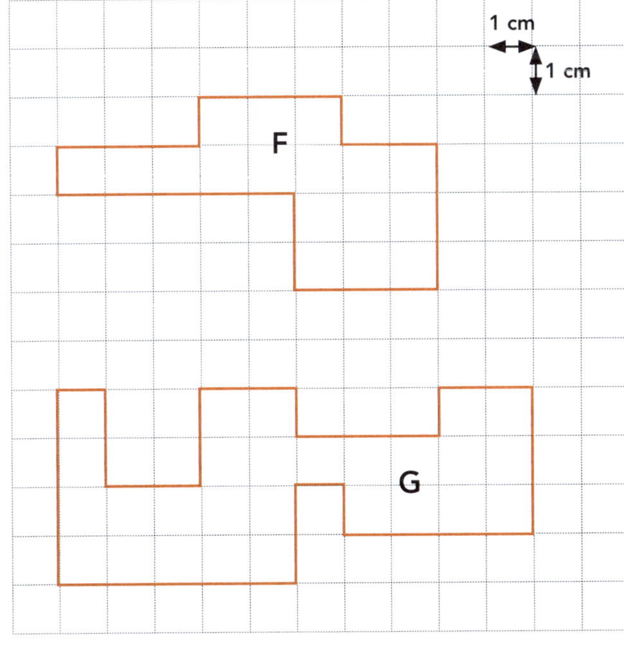

F = ______________________

____

____

____

G = ______________________

____

____

____

ISBN: 9780170447171

Shapes with linear sides

- Remember, to find the perimeter you need to **start at one corner** and **add** the distances around the outside of the shape.

Examples:

1

All the sides are the same, because this is a square.

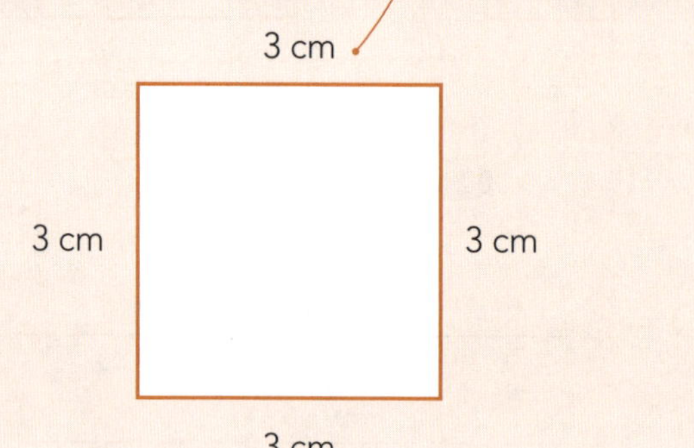

Perimeter = 3 + 3 + 3 + 3
= 12 cm

2

Make sure you remember where you started by using a dot.

Perimeter = 4 + 6 + 3
= 13 m

Calculate the perimeters of these shapes.

1

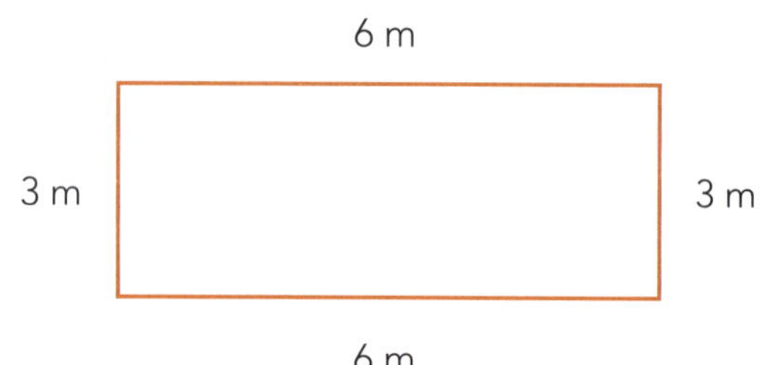

2

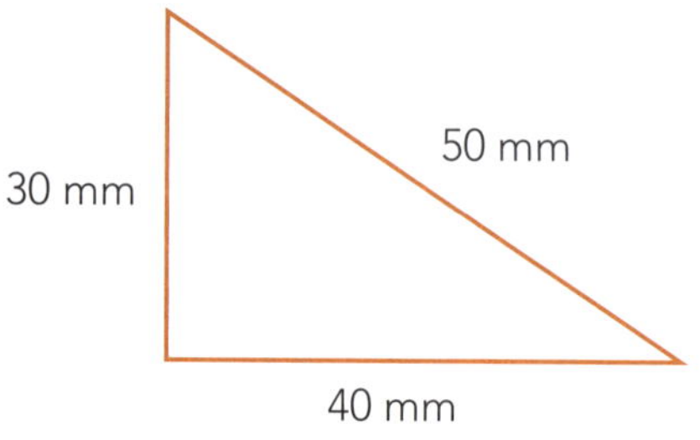

3

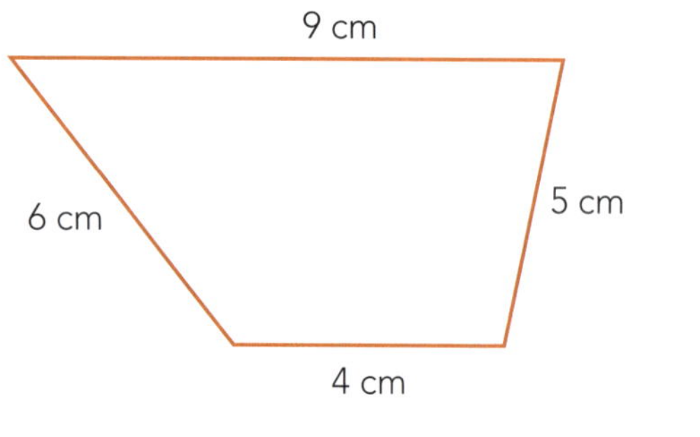

4

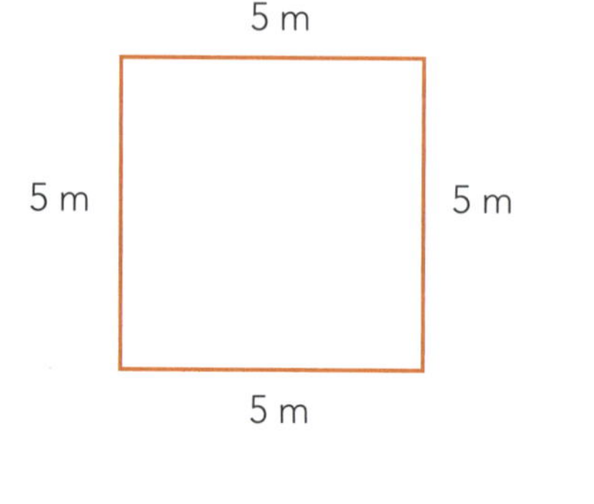

 ISBN: 9780170447171

5

4 km
5 km
2 km
4 km
4 km

6

5 m
2 m
2 m
5 m

7

40 mm
20 mm
15 mm
30 mm
35 mm

8

9 cm
14 cm
5 cm
16 cm

9

2 m
2 m
2 m
3 m
3 m
2 m
2 m
2 m

10

2.5 km
3.5 km
1.5 km
1 km
1 km
2 km
2 km
1 km

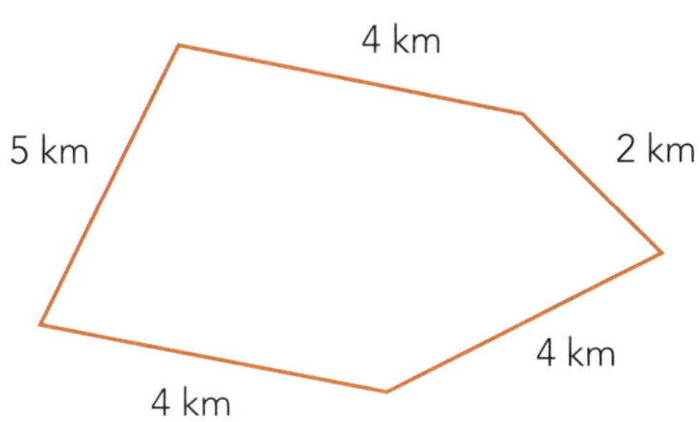

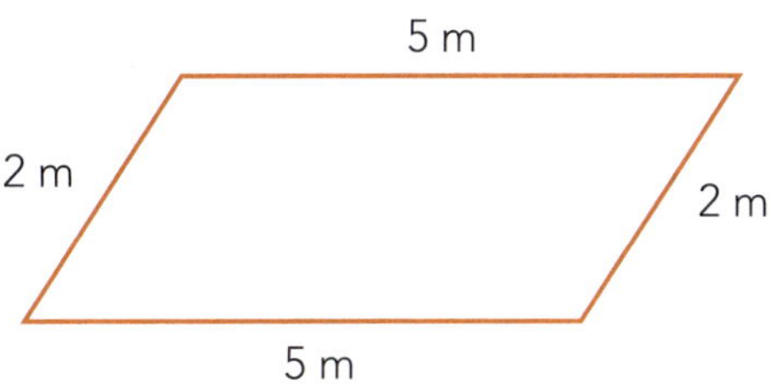

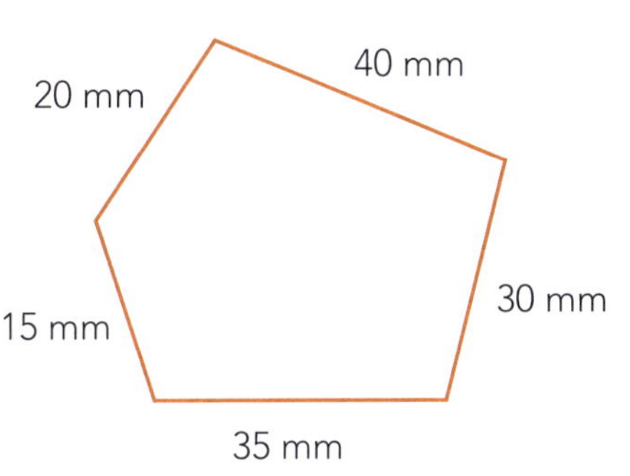

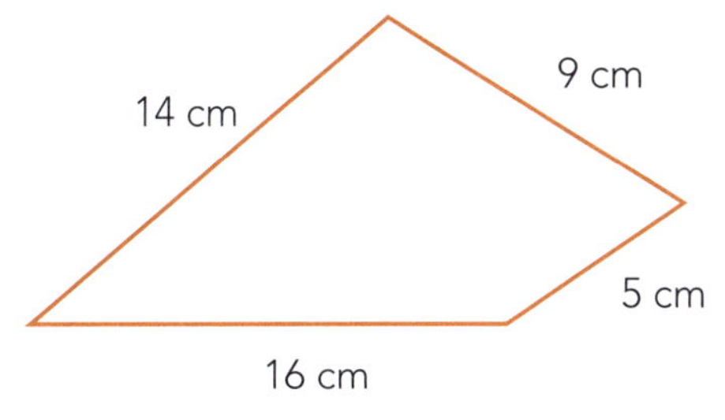

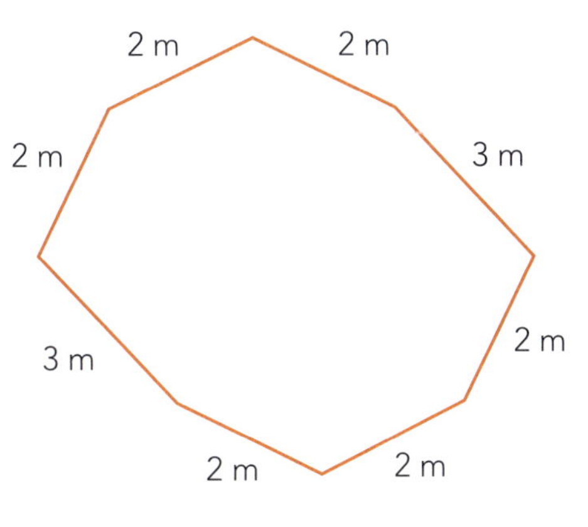

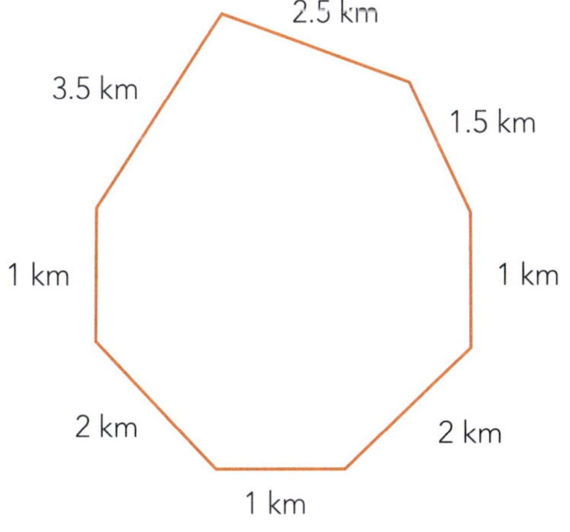

Symbols on diagrams

- Some shapes don't have numbers on each side, but instead they have a symbol that indicates it is the same value as another side.
- It is a good idea to write these values on the diagram.
- Remember to mark your starting point with a dot.

Examples:

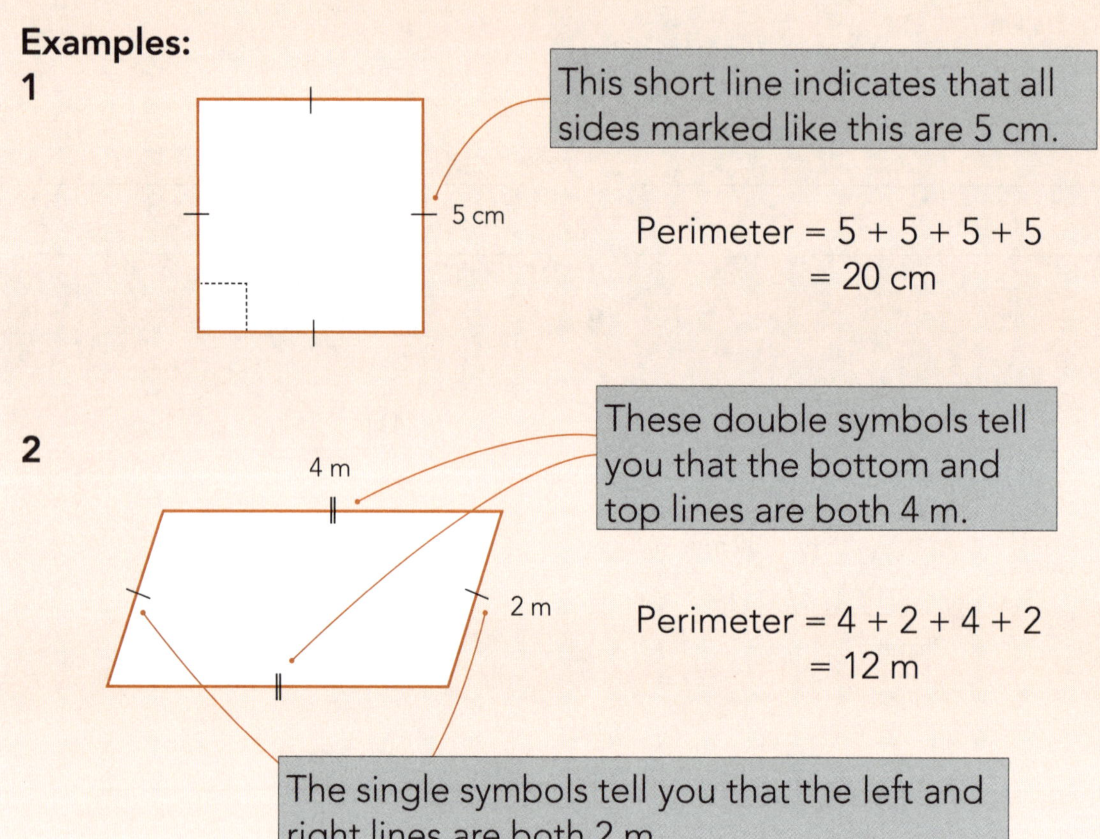

Calculate the perimeters of these shapes.

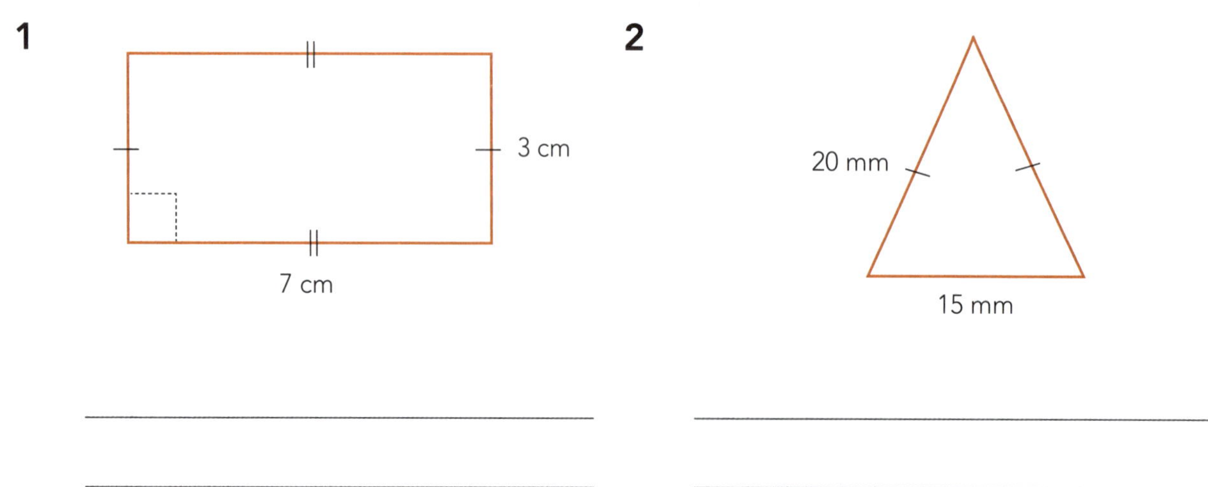

 ISBN: 9780170447171

3

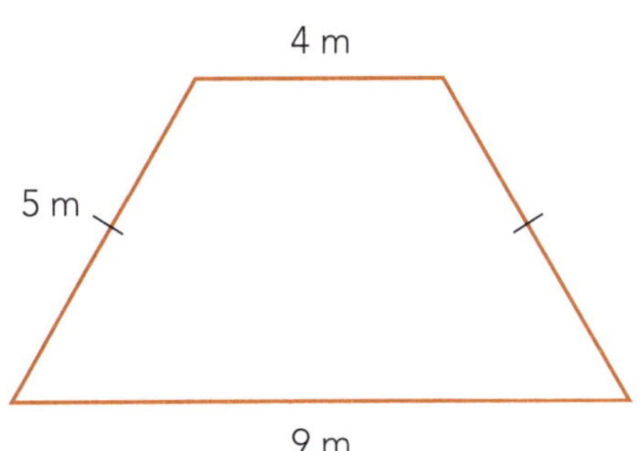

4

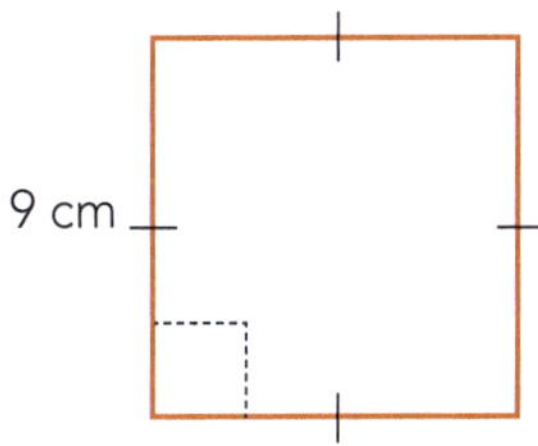

5

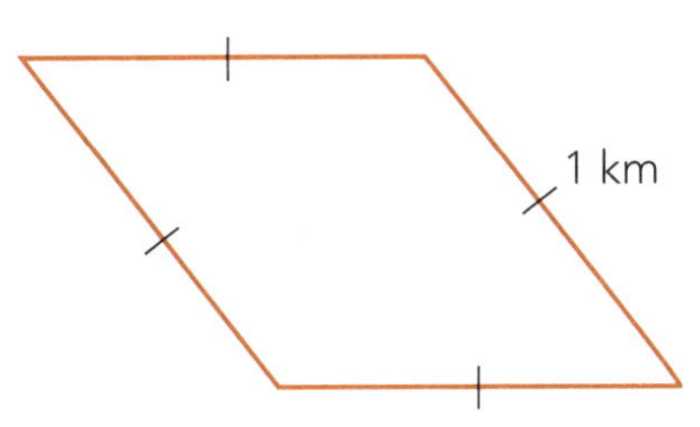

6

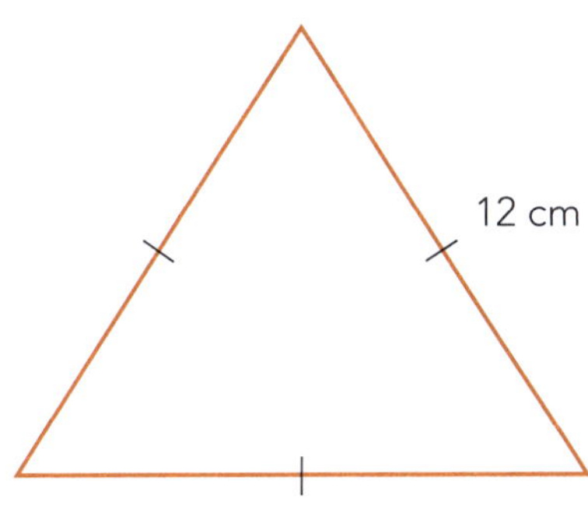

7

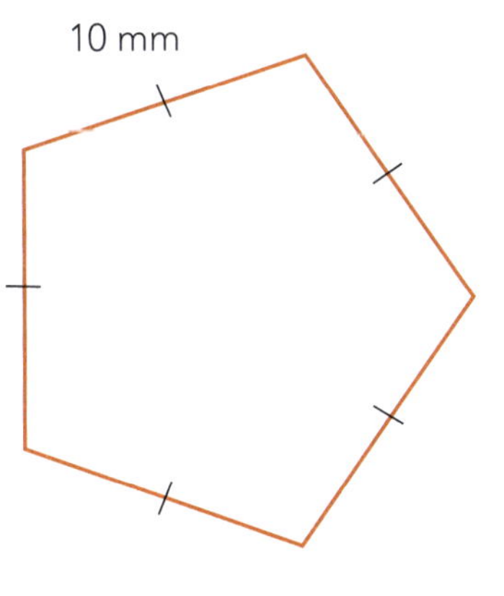

8

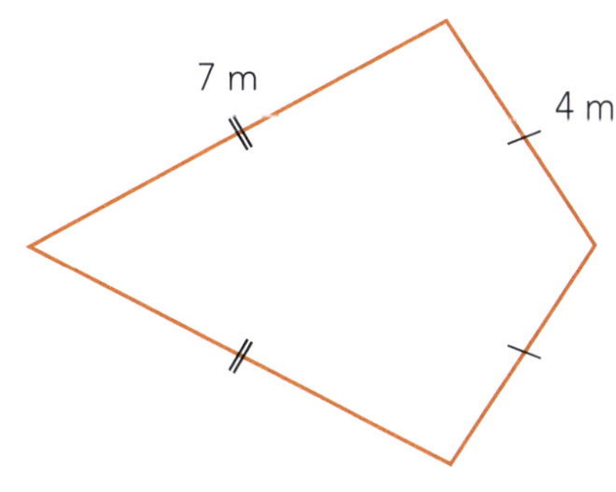

ISBN: 9780170447171

Things to look out for

Regular shapes

- 'Regular' means all the sides are the same length. In this case, each side is 8 mm long.

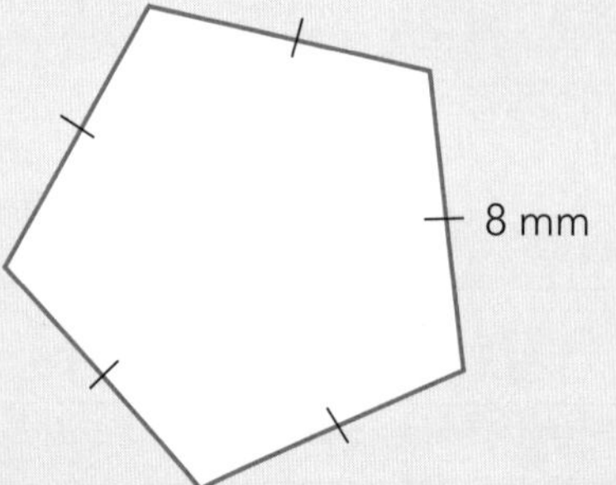

Perimeter = 8 + 8 + 8 + 8 + 8
= 5 x 8
= 40 mm

Extra measurements

- There may be measurements that are not needed for calculating the perimeter.

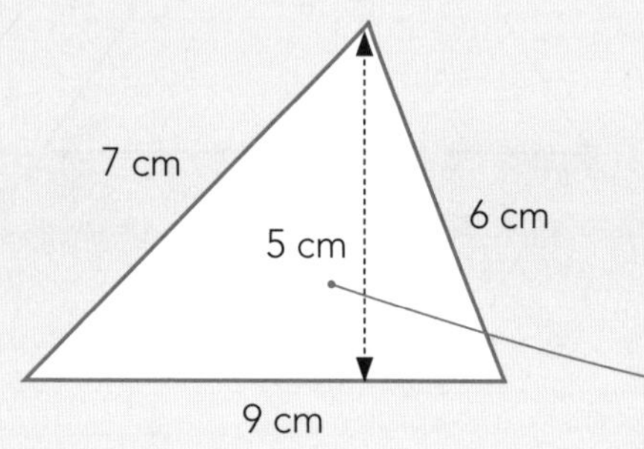

Perimeter = 6 + 9 + 7
= 22 cm

The 5 cm is not needed in order to calculate the perimeter.

Different units

- Some shapes may have measurements with different units.
- You need to make sure that all the information you need is in the same units before calculating the perimeter.

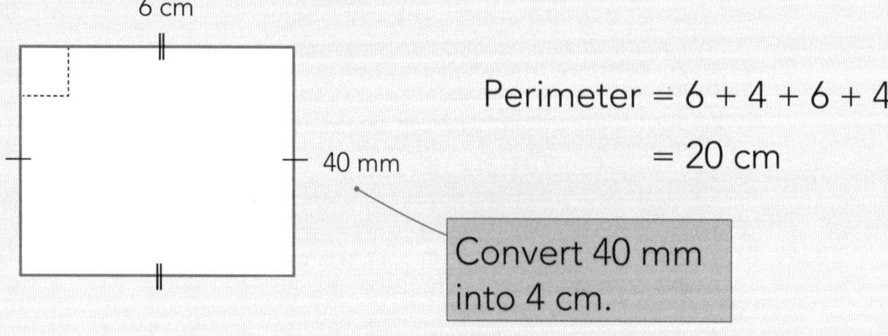

Perimeter = 6 + 4 + 6 + 4
= 20 cm

Convert 40 mm into 4 cm.

ISBN: 9780170447171

Calculate the perimeters of these shapes.

1 This is a regular hexagon.

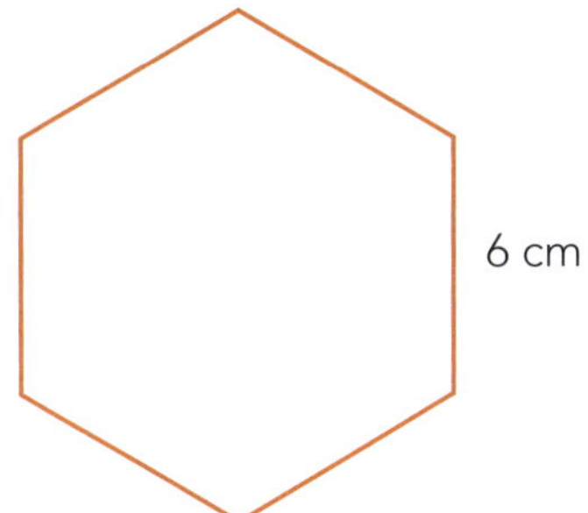

2

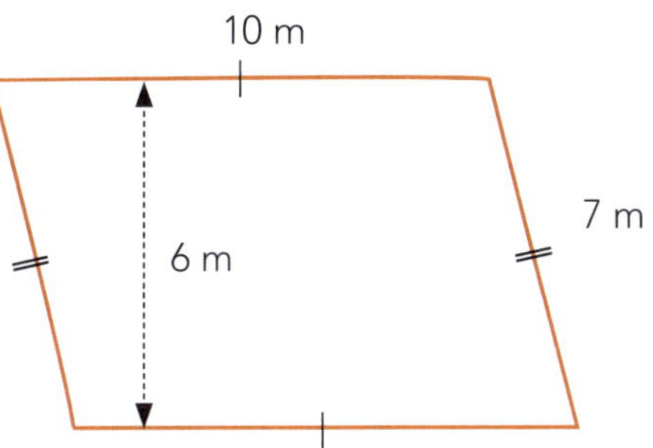

3 Write your answer in metres (m).

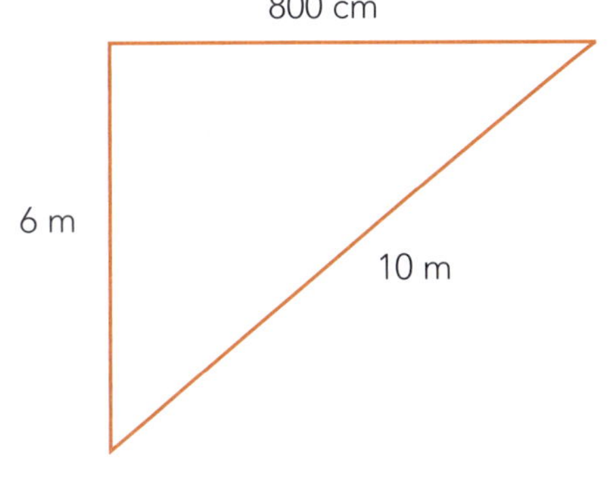

4 This is a regular octagon.

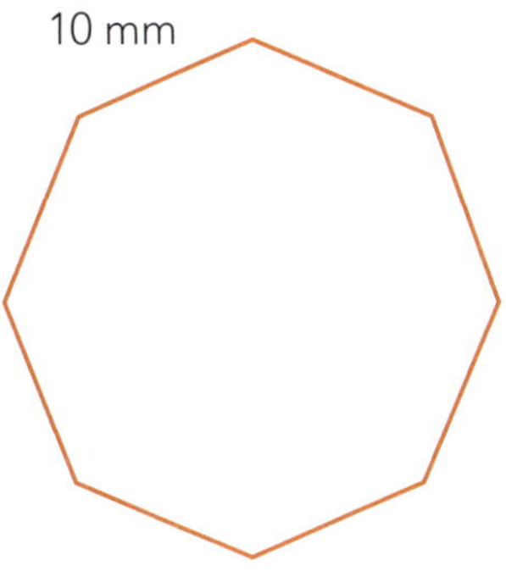

5

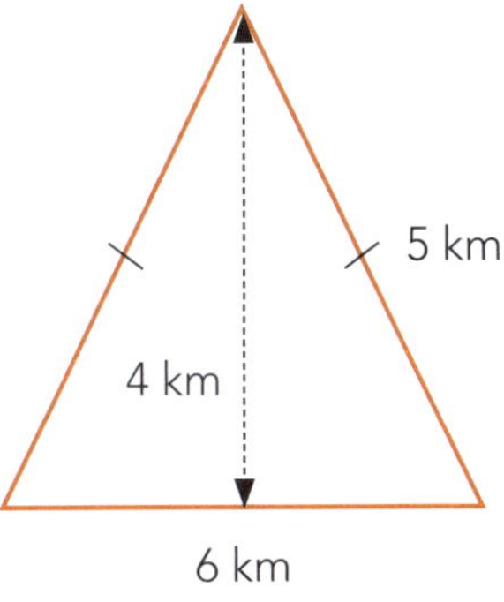

6 Write your answer in metres (m).

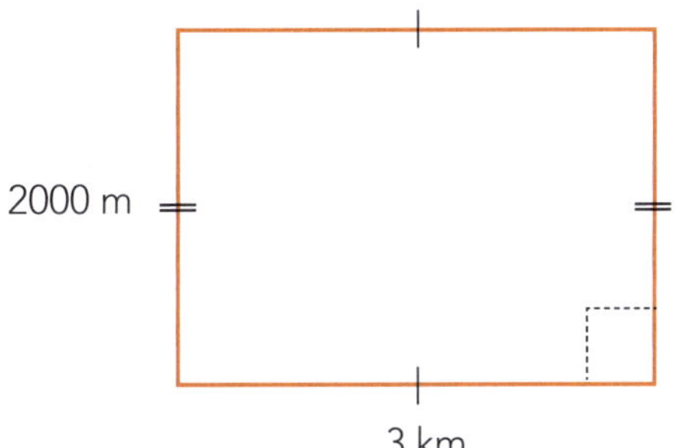

7 This is a regular heptagon.

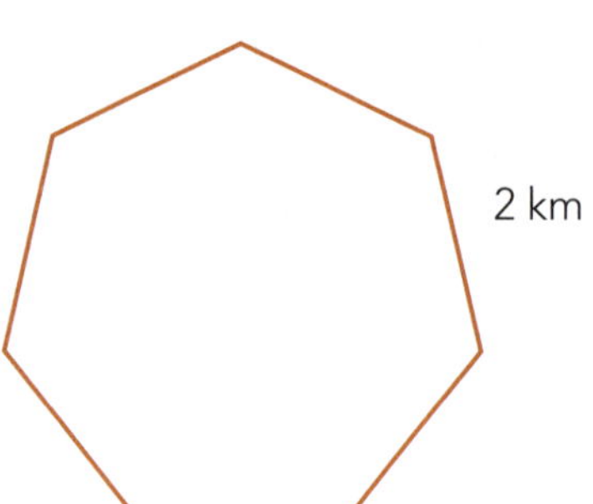

8

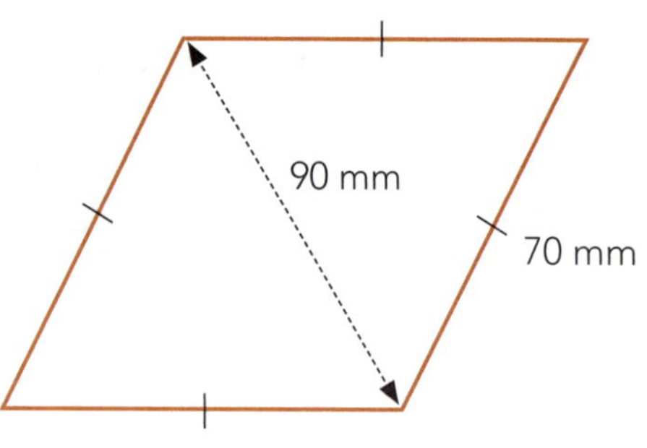

9 Write your answer in kilometres (km).

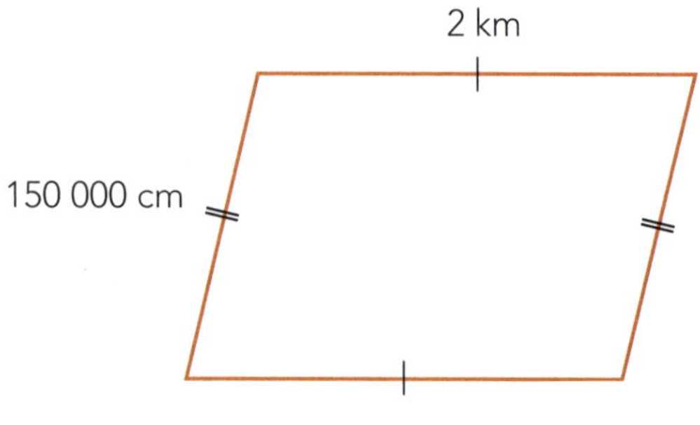

10 Write your answer in centimetres (cm).

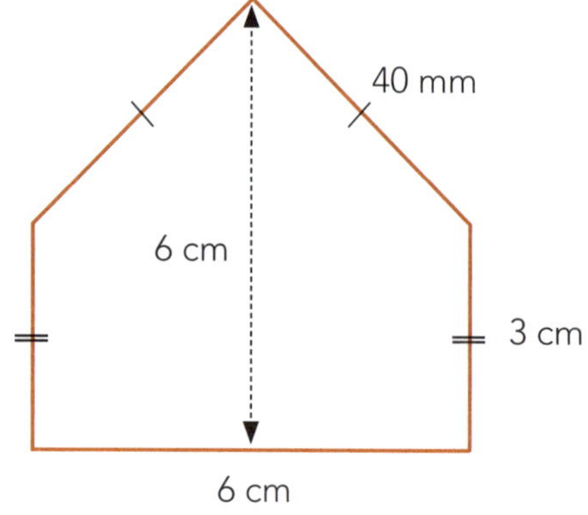

11 Write your answer in centimetres (cm).

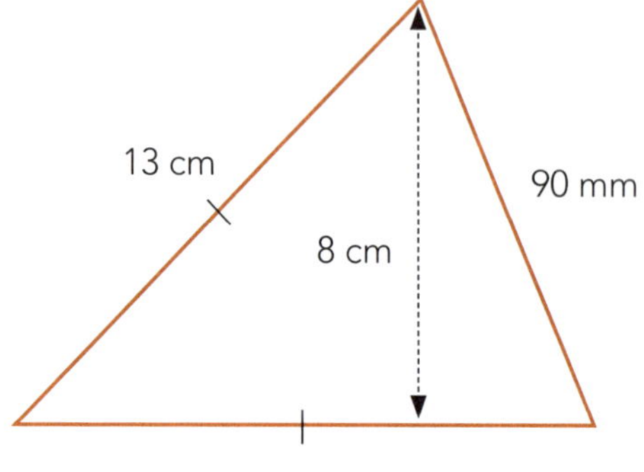

12 This is a regular pentagon.

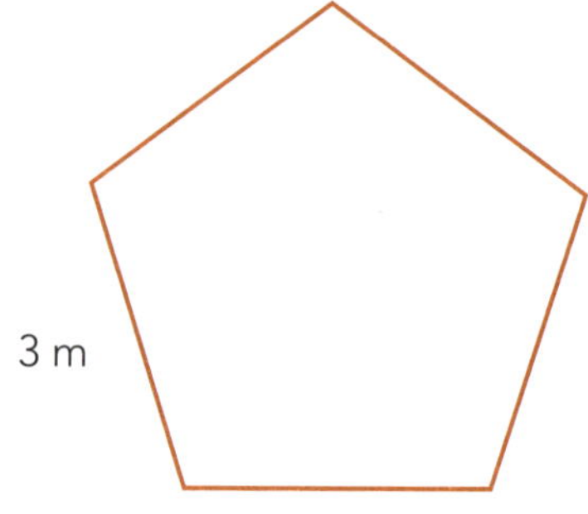

 ISBN: 9780170447171

Working backwards

- Sometimes you may be given the perimeter and asked to work backwards to find a missing length.

Examples:

1 This triangle has a perimeter of 12 km.

4 km

?

5 km

Calculate the missing length.

Perimeter = side 1 + side 2 + side 3

$12 = 4 + 5 + ?$

$12 = 9 + ?$

Ask yourself, '9 plus what equals 12?'

The missing length must be 3 km.

2 This rectangle has a perimeter of 28 cm. The base of it is 10 cm. Calculate its height, h.

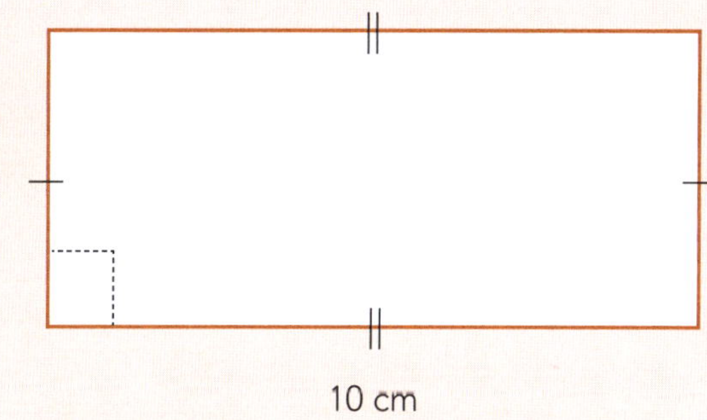

Perimeter = $h + h + b + b$

$28 = h + h + 10 + 10$

$28 = h + h + 20$

Ask yourself, '20 plus what equals 28?'

$28 = 8 + 20$

$28 = \mathbf{4 + 4} + 20$

We must split the 8 in two because there are two heights.

The missing height must be 4 cm.

ISBN: 9780170447171

Answer the following questions.

1 The perimeter of this triangle is 19 m. Calculate the length of the third side.

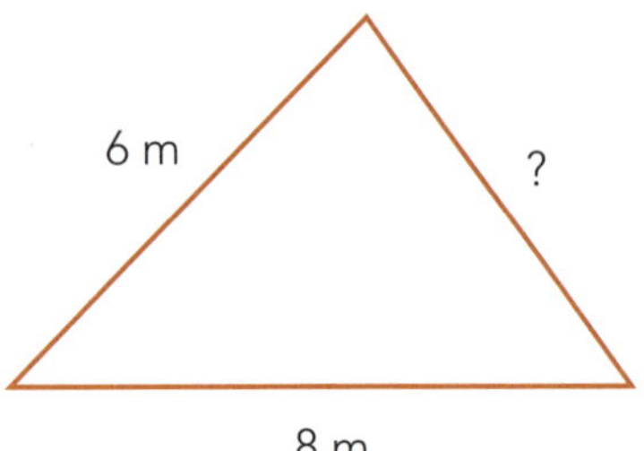

2 The perimeter of this rectangle is 24 mm. Calculate its height.

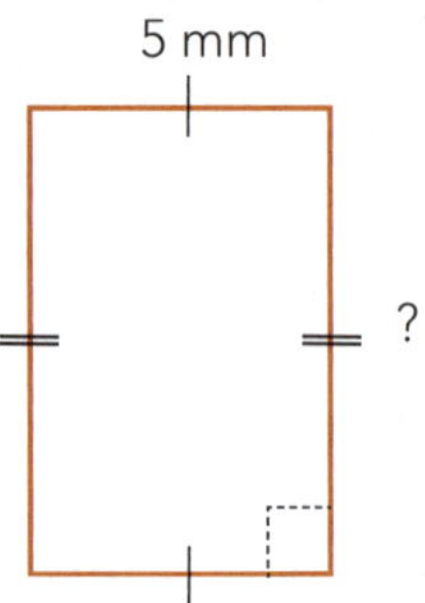

3 The perimeter of this isosceles triangle is 16 km. Calculate the missing side lengths.

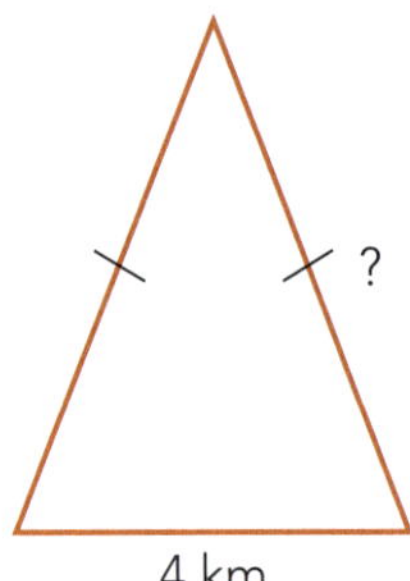

4 The perimeter of this square is 64 cm. Calculate the length of its sides.

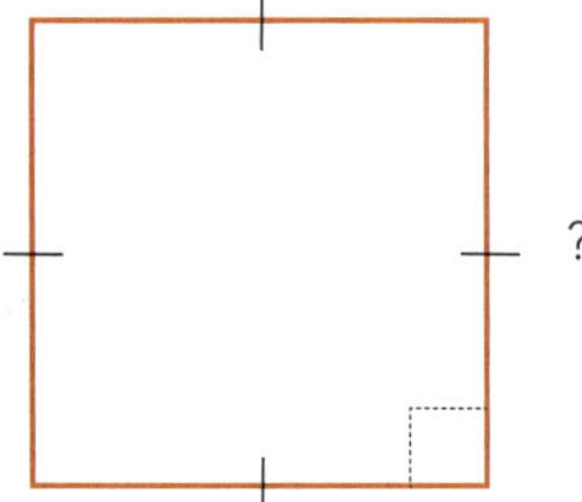

5 The perimeter of this pentagon is 6 km. Find the length of each side.

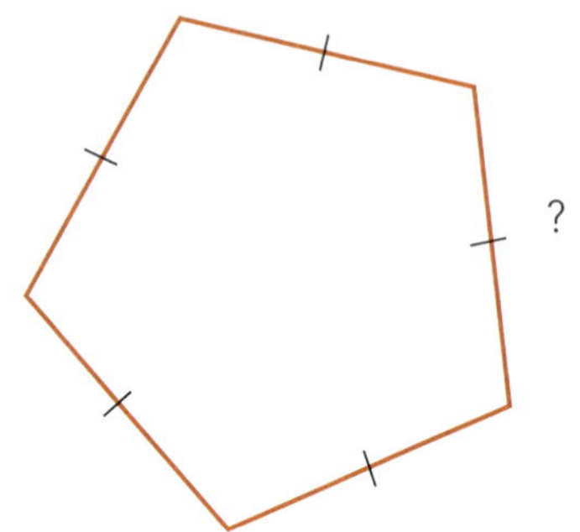

6 The perimeter of this triangle is 15 cm. Find the length of the third side in centimetres (cm).

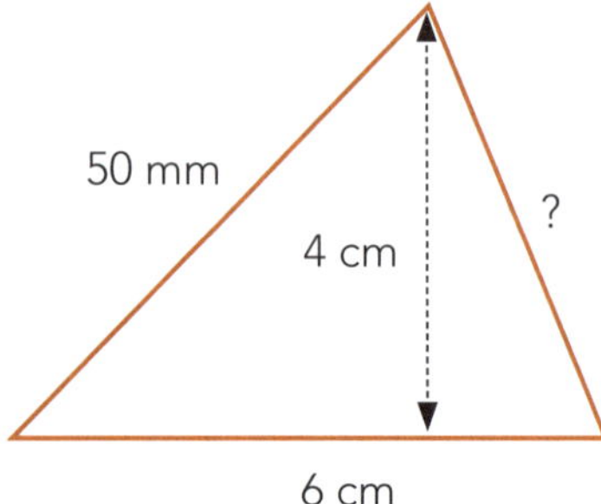

 ISBN: 9780170447171

Compound shapes

- A compound shape is a shape made up of **several 'basic' shapes**.
- Remember to mark your starting point with a dot.

Calculate the perimeters of these compound shapes.

1

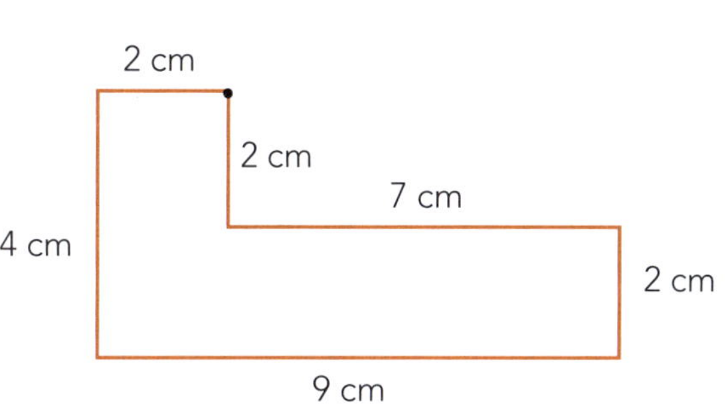

____

____

2

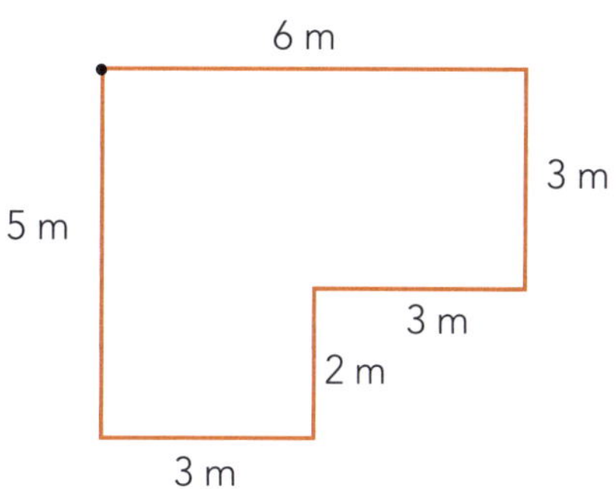

____

____

3

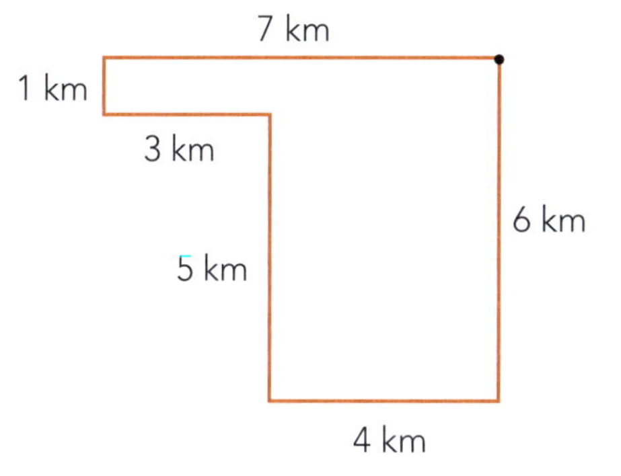

____

____

4

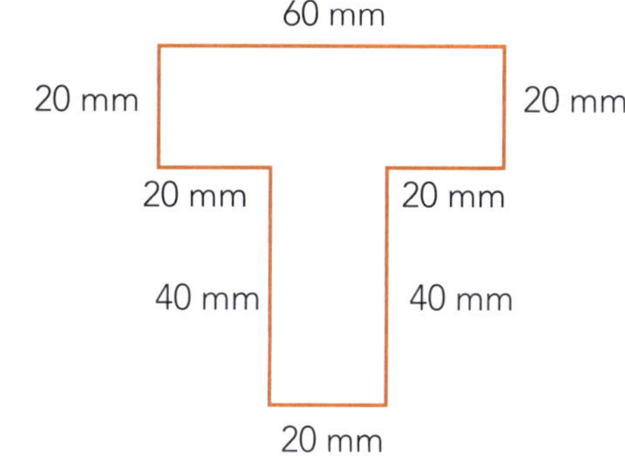

____

____

5

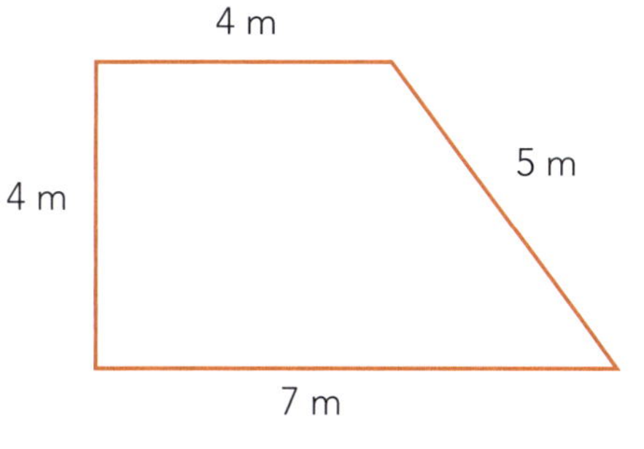

____

____

6

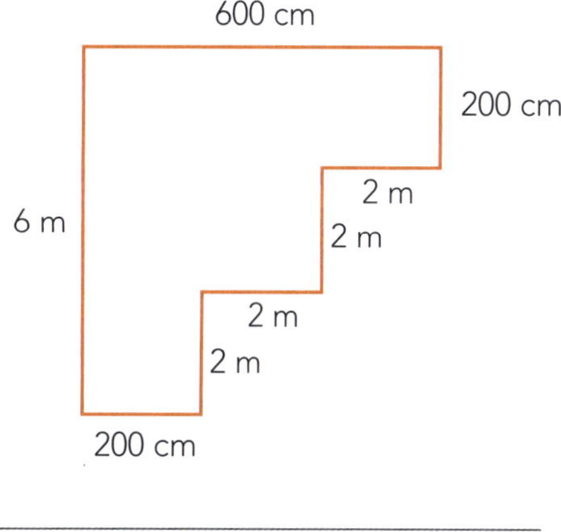

____

____

ISBN: 9780170447171

Compound shapes with missing measurements

- Not all measurements may be written on diagrams, so you will need to calculate some.
- It's a good idea to add these to the diagram before you calculate the answer.
- Remember to mark your starting point with a dot.

Example:

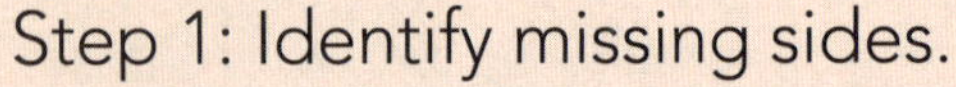
Step 1: Identify missing sides.

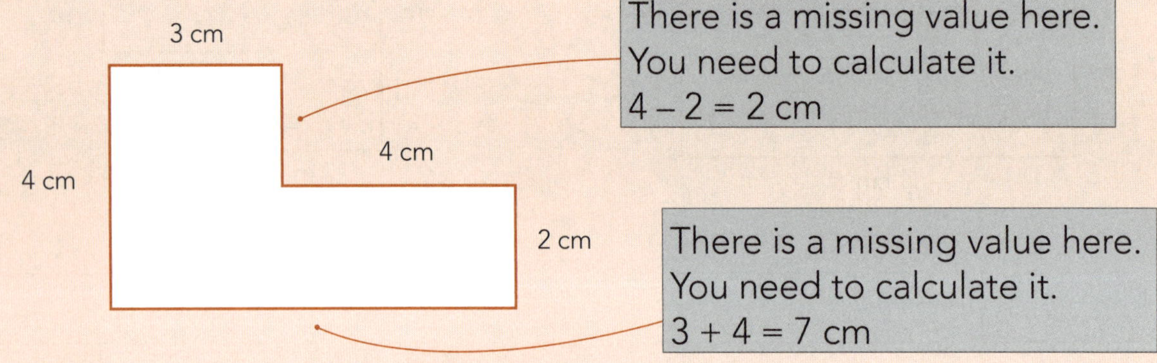

Step 2: Add values to your diagram.

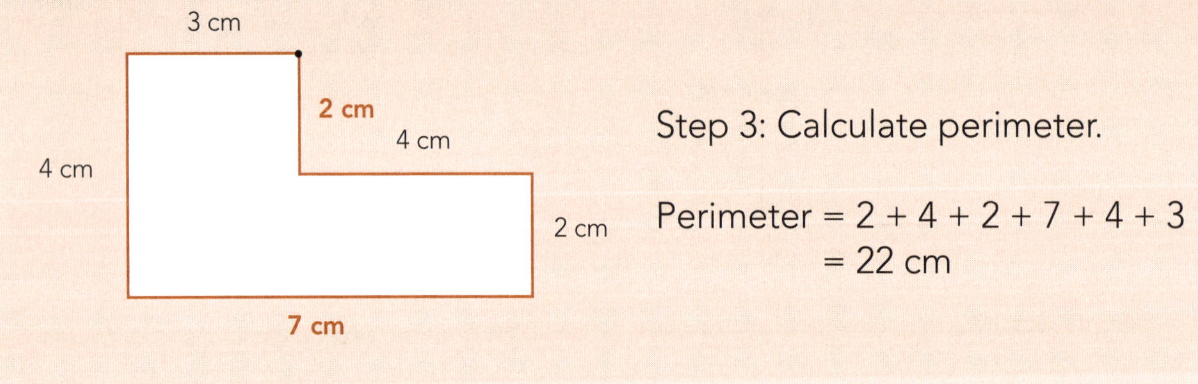

Step 3: Calculate perimeter.

Perimeter = 2 + 4 + 2 + 7 + 4 + 3
= 22 cm

Calculate the perimeters of these compound shapes.

1

?
2 m
5 m
3 m
?
2 m

____

____

____

ISBN: 9780170447171

2

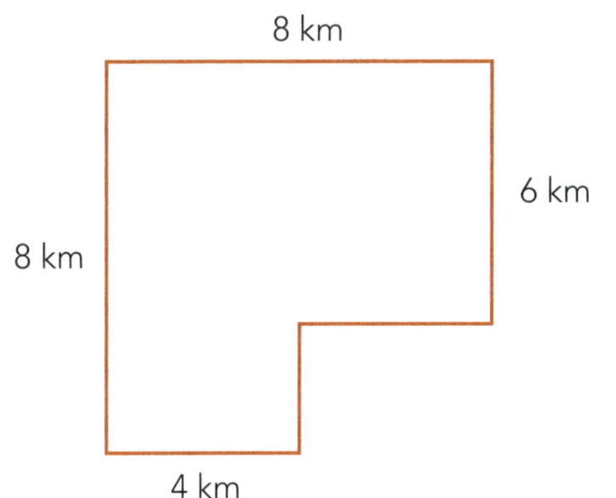

3

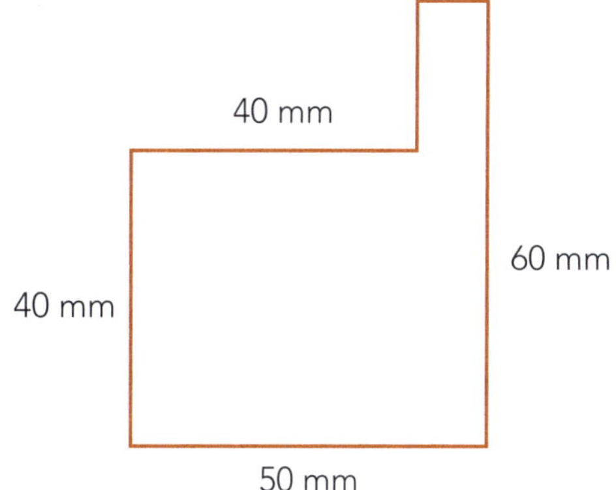

4

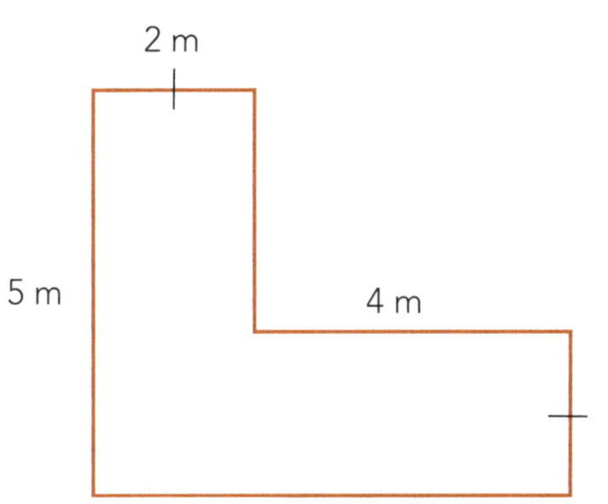

5

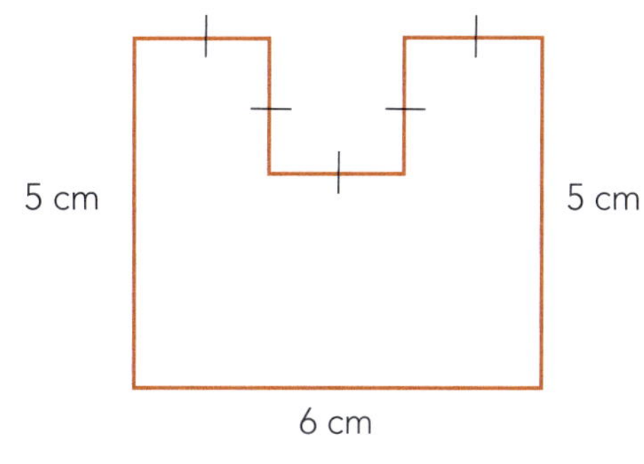

6

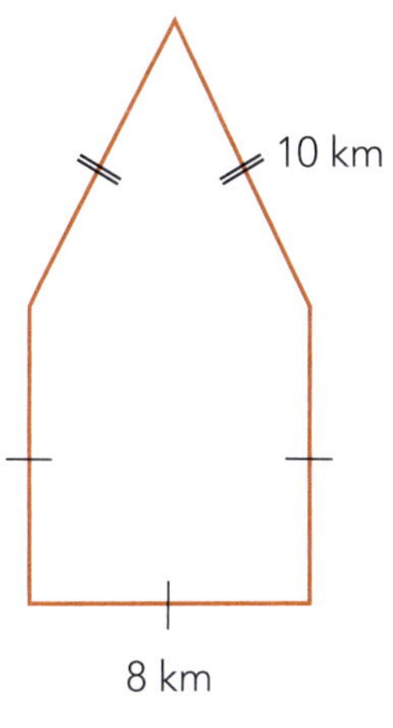

7

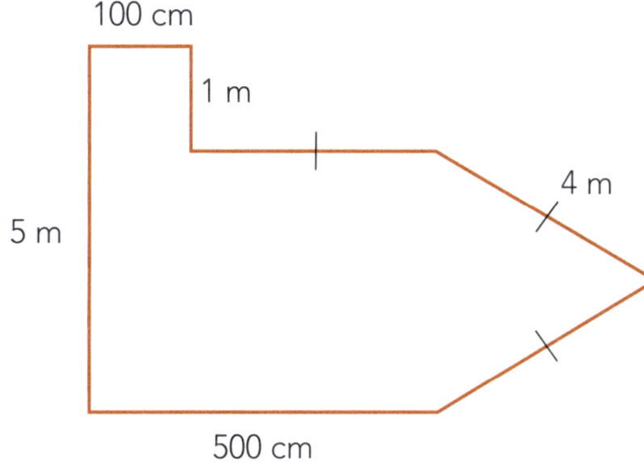

ISBN: 9780170447171

Word questions

Word questions are easier if you follow these steps:

Step 1: Identify the shape.

Step 2: Sketch a diagram.

Step 3: Add the measurements to the diagram.

Step 4: Calculate the perimeter.

Example:

A rectangular box measures 12 cm by 8 cm. Calculate its perimeter.

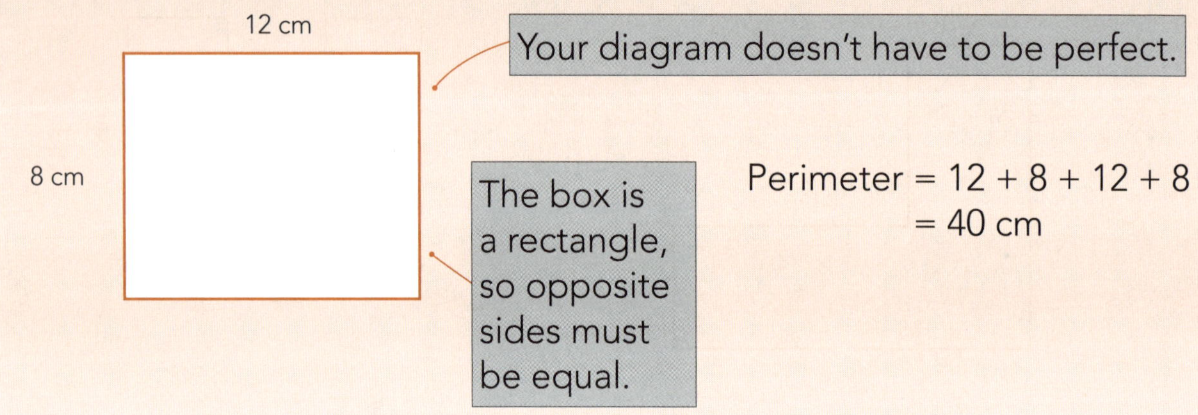

Answer the following questions.

1 Each side of a square table is 2 m long. What is the perimeter of the table?

2 The sides of a parallelogram are 40 mm and 35 mm. Calculate its perimeter.

ISBN: 9780170447171

3 Sarah is running around the local park. Its three sides are 4 km, 5 km and 3 km. How far does she run?

4 The sides of an equilateral triangle have a total length of 33 cm. How long is each side?

5 A square has a perimeter of 60 m. How long is each side?

6 What is the perimeter of a regular octagon with 12 cm sides?

7 The short side of an isoceles triangle is 4 m long, and its perimeter is 22 m. How long is each of the other two sides?

8 A rhombus has sides of 200 cm and 2 m. What is its perimeter?

ISBN: 9780170447171

Challenge 1

Calculate the perimeter of these shapes.

1

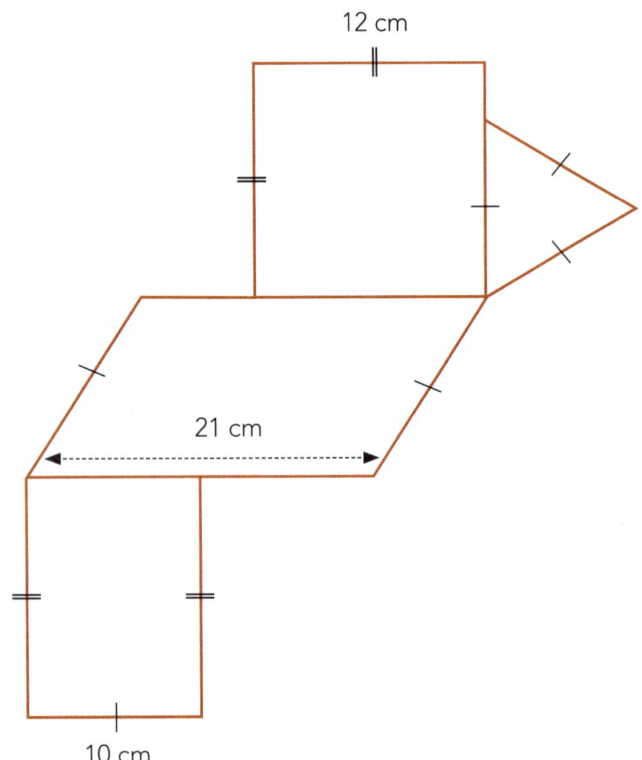

2

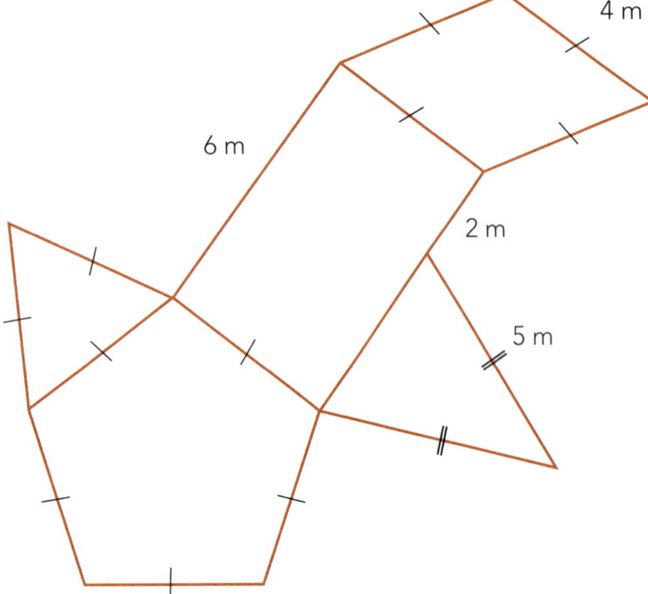

 ISBN: 9780170447171

Area

Shapes on a grid

If you can **paint** it, it's area.

- The area is the size of a **flat surface** inside a two-dimensional (2D) shape.
- To calculate the area of shapes on grids, **count the number of squares** inside each.
- The shapes are drawn on a 1 cm by 1 cm grid.

Examples:

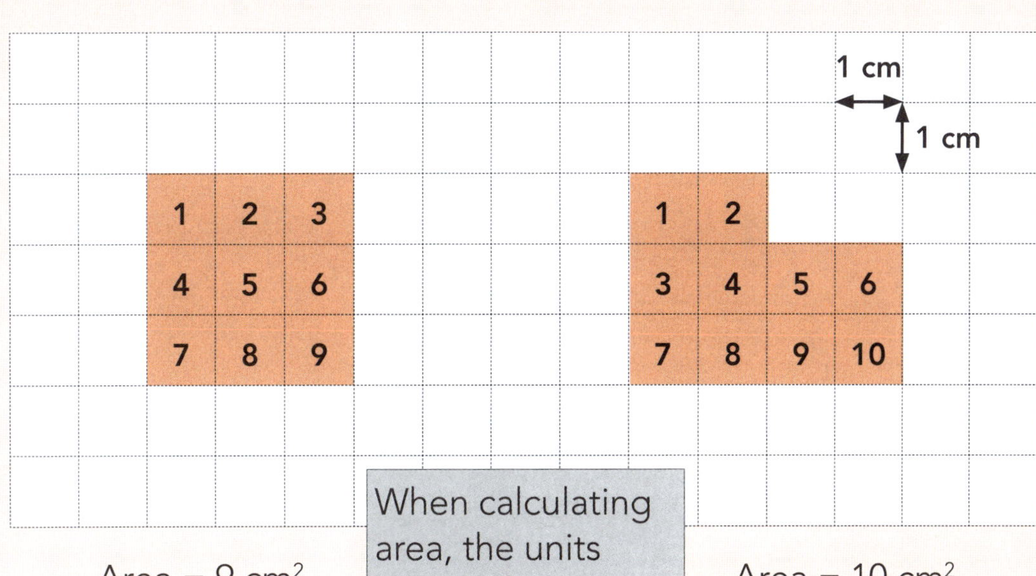

Area = 9 cm^2

When calculating area, the units have ^{2} after them.

Area = 10 cm^2

Find the areas of these shapes.

1

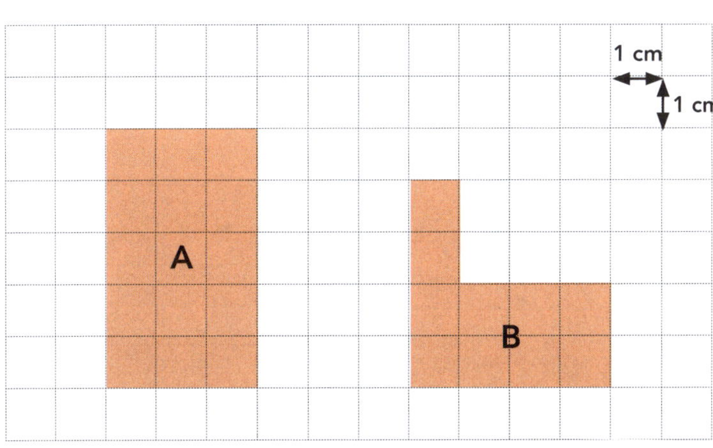

A = ______________________

____

B = ______________________

____

ISBN: 9780170447171

2

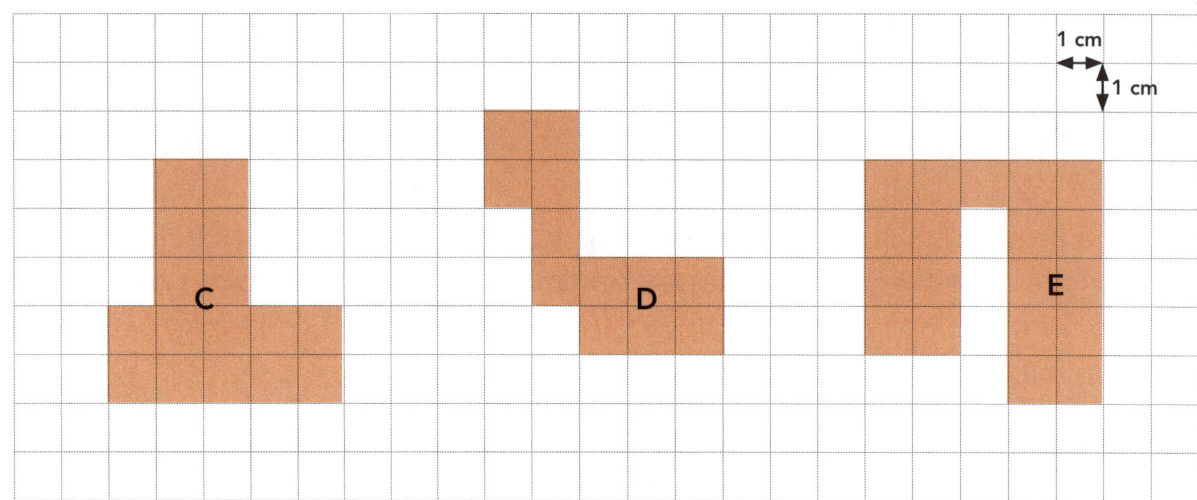

C = ______________________
____

D = ______________________
____

E = ______________________
____

3

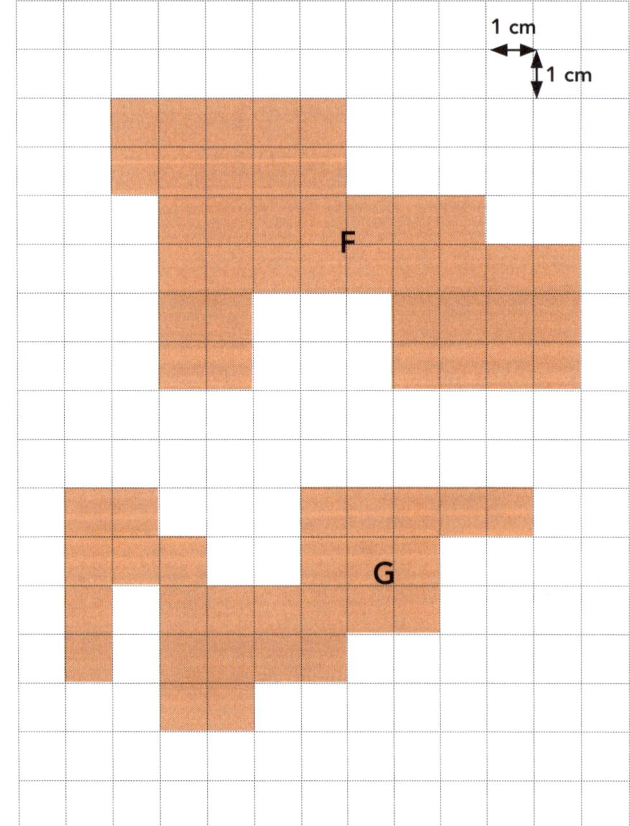

F = ______________________
____
____
____

G = ______________________
____
____
____

 ISBN: 9780170447171

Rectangles on a grid

- Rectangles with the same area can be drawn different ways.

Example:
These rectangles all have an area of 12 cm^2.

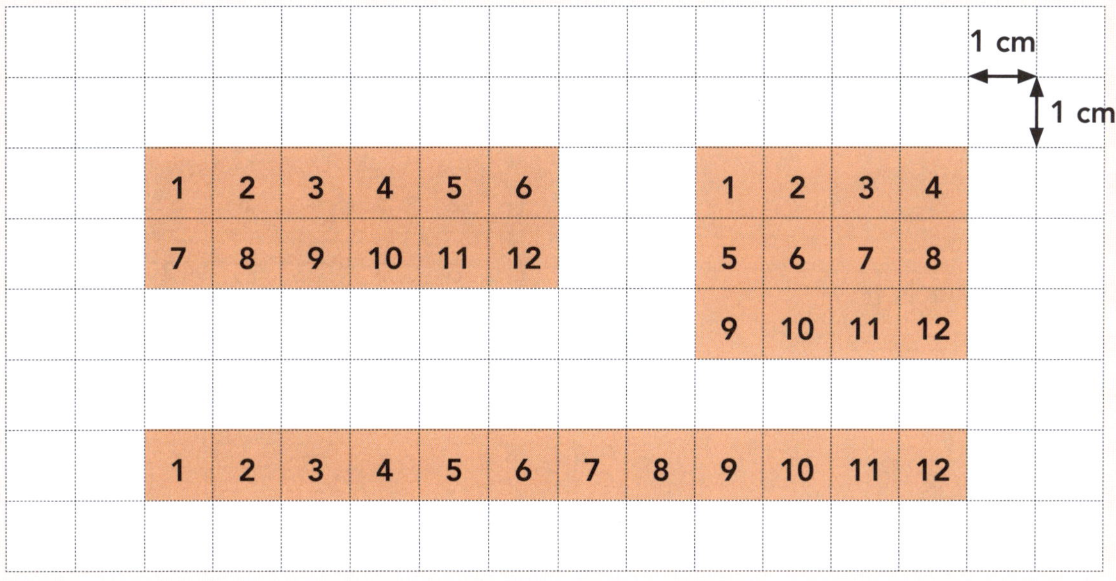

Sketch the four different ways of constructing rectangles with an area of 24 cm^2. The sides must be whole numbers.

Rectangles using the formula

- Using the formula is a more efficient way of finding areas rather than counting squares.

Example:
These rectangles both have an area of 12 cm^2.

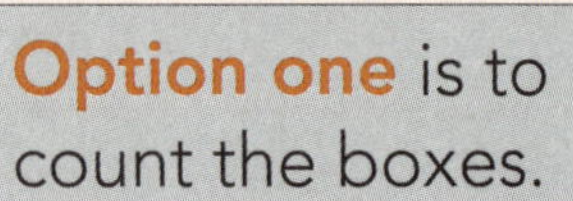

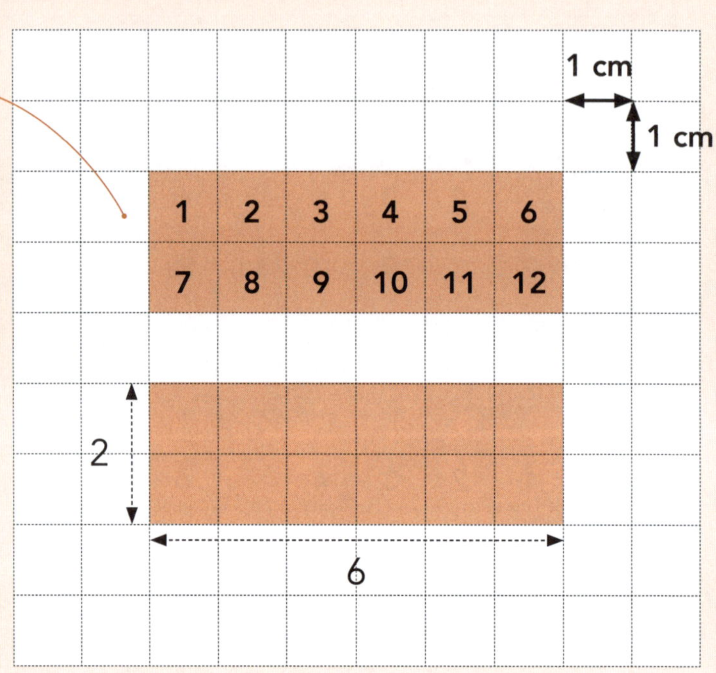

Option two is to multiply the base by the height.

Area = base x height
= 6 x 2
= 12 cm^2

Use the formula to calculate the area of these two rectangles, then check your answer by counting the squares.

1

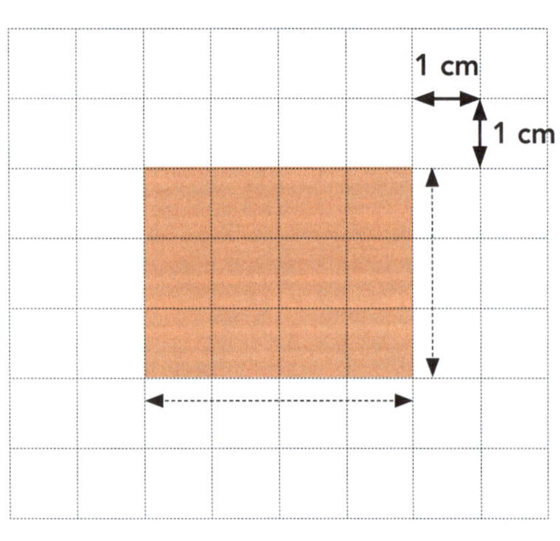

____

____

2

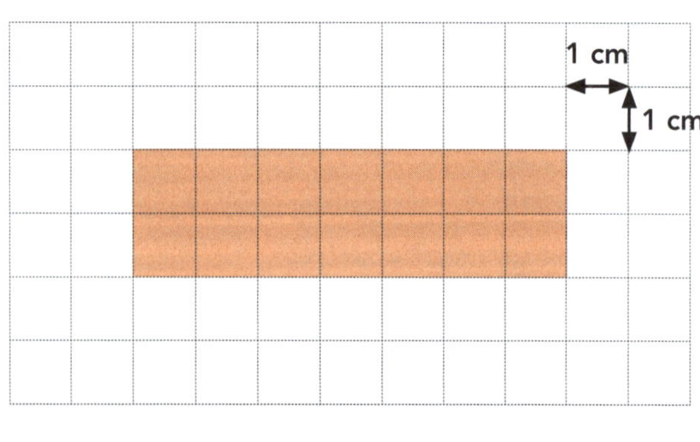

____

____

ISBN: 9780170447171

Quadrilaterals

Square and rectangle

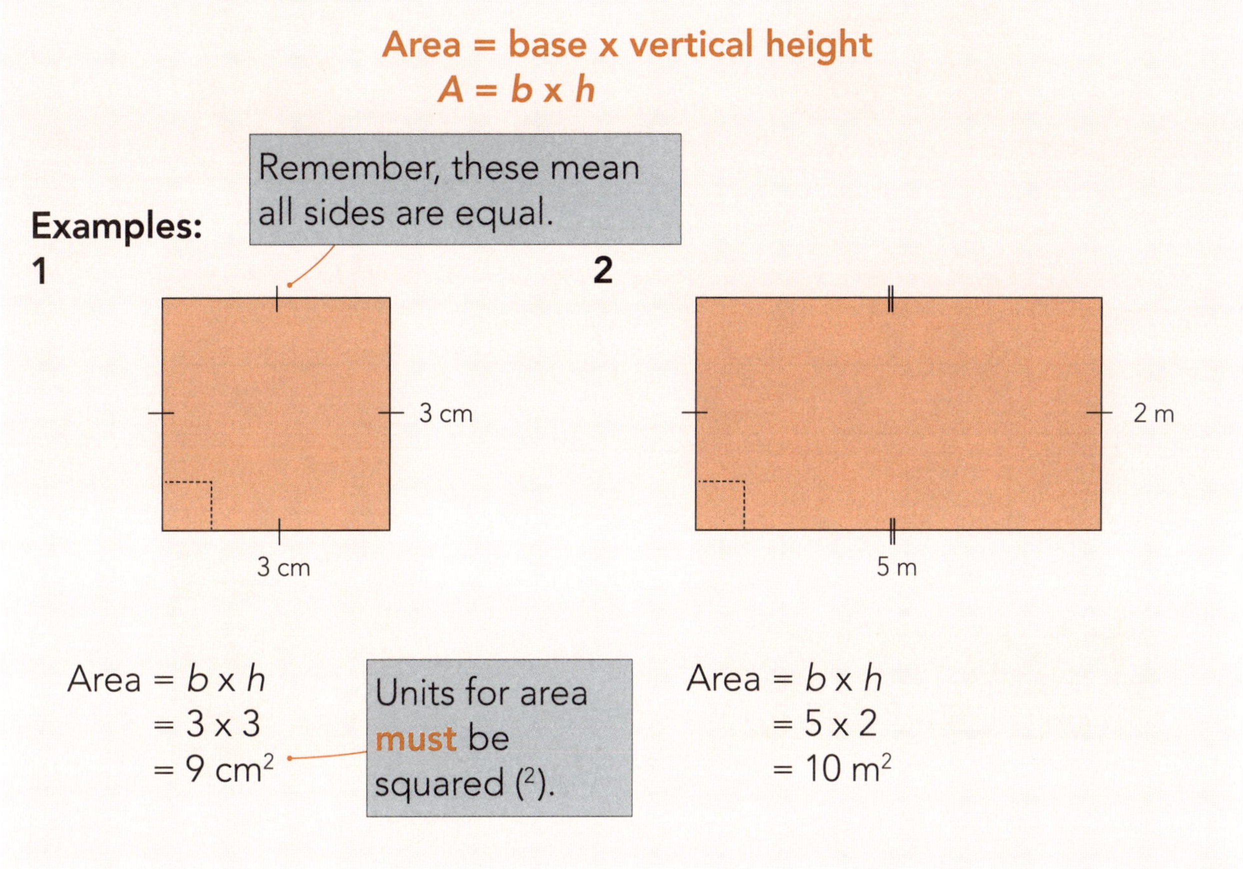

Calculate the areas of these shapes.

1

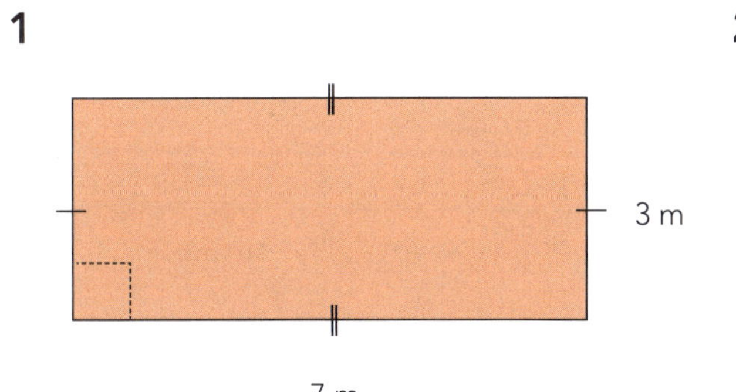

2

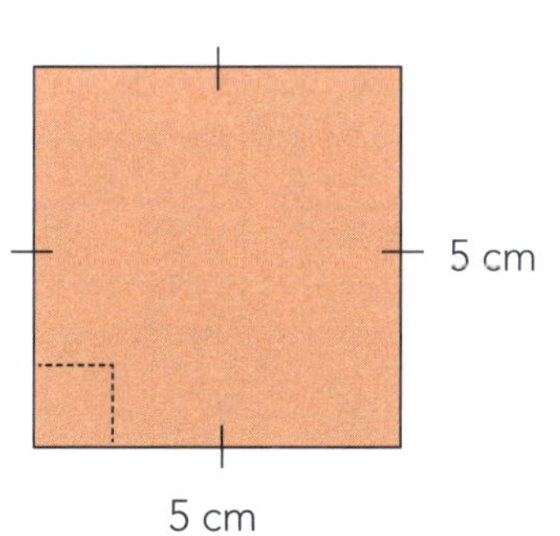

ISBN: 9780170447171

3

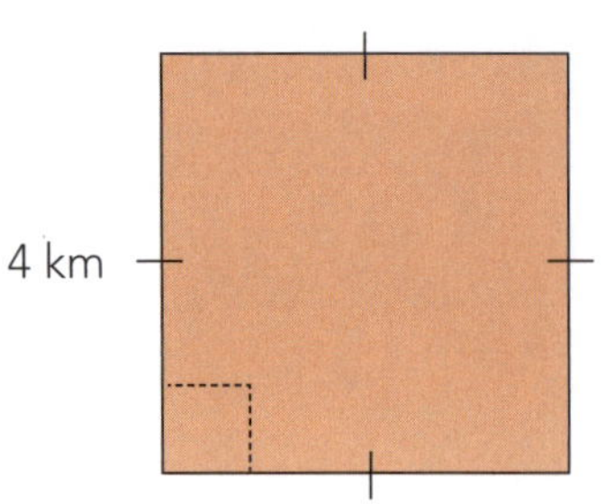

4

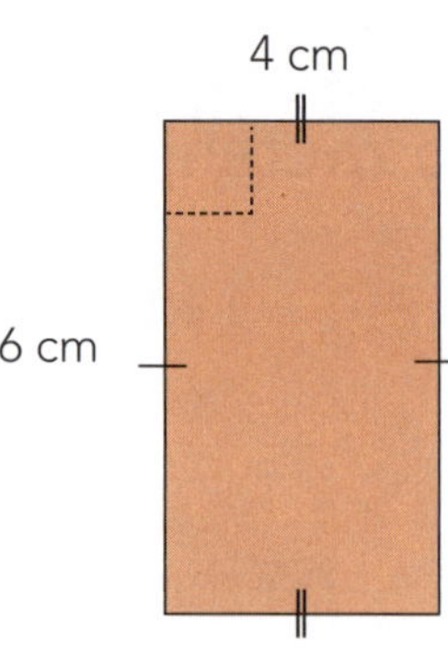

5

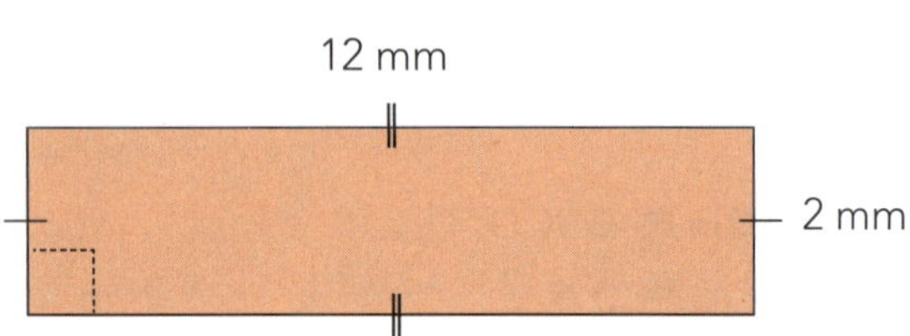

6

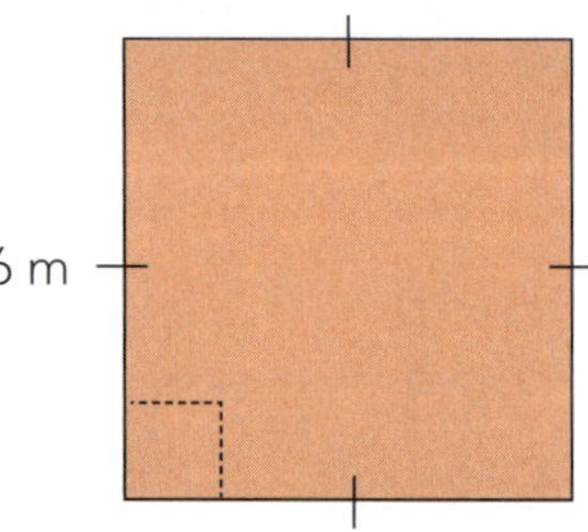

7

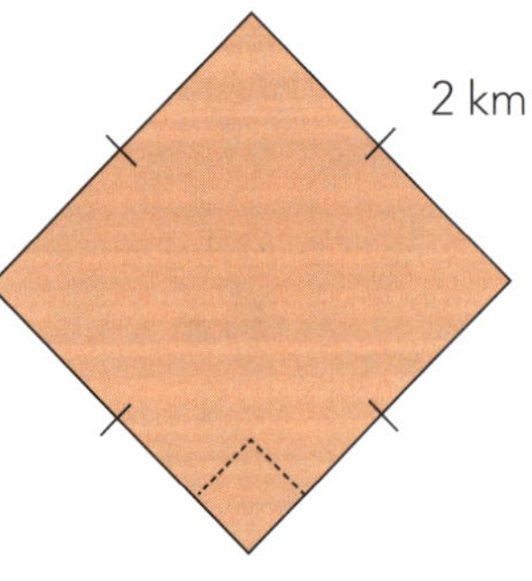

8

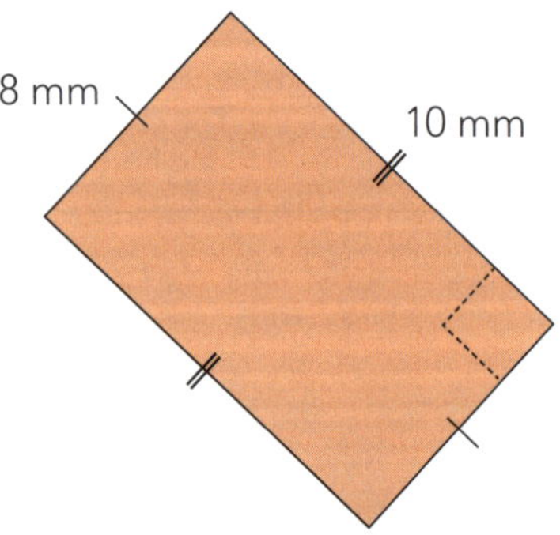

 ISBN: 9780170447171

Parallelogram and rhombus

- A **parallelogram** has opposite sides that are parallel and equal.
- A **rhombus** has four equal sides, and opposite sides are parallel.

You can rearrange a parallelogram to look like a rectangle.

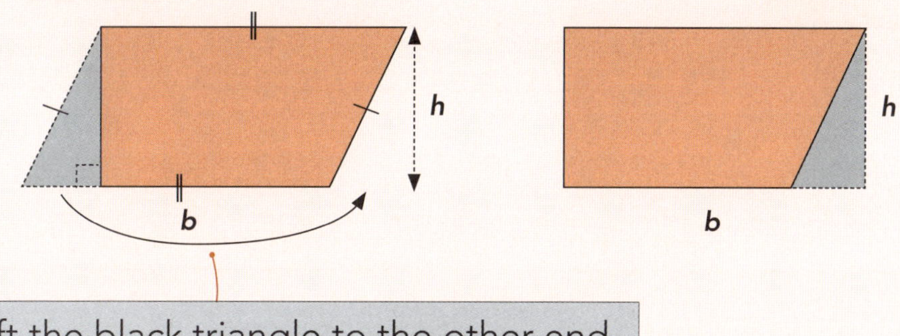

Shift the black triangle to the other end.

So the formula stays the same: **Area = base x vertical height**

$A = b \times h$

Examples:

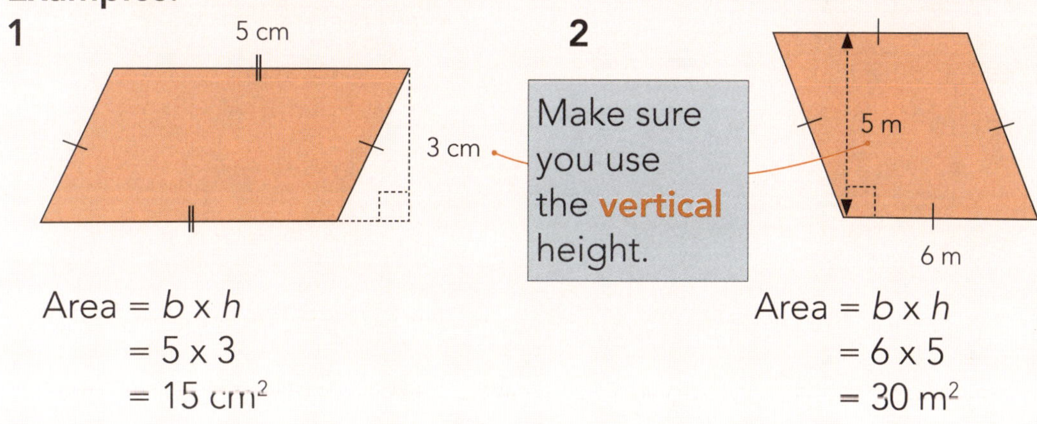

1

Area $= b \times h$
$= 5 \times 3$
$= 15\ \text{cm}^2$

2

Area $= b \times h$
$= 6 \times 5$
$= 30\ \text{m}^2$

Calculate the areas of these shapes.

1

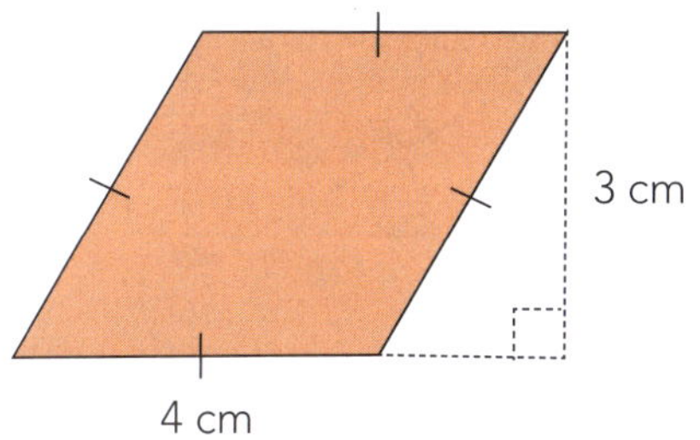

2

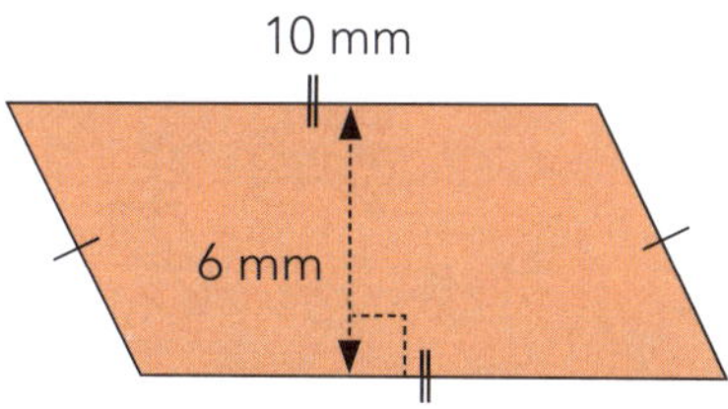

3

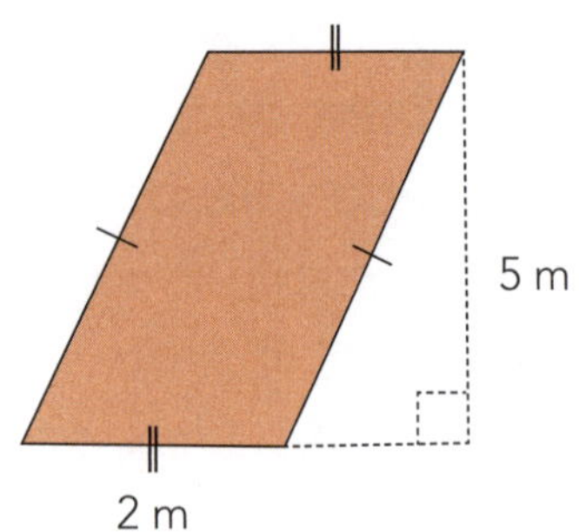

4

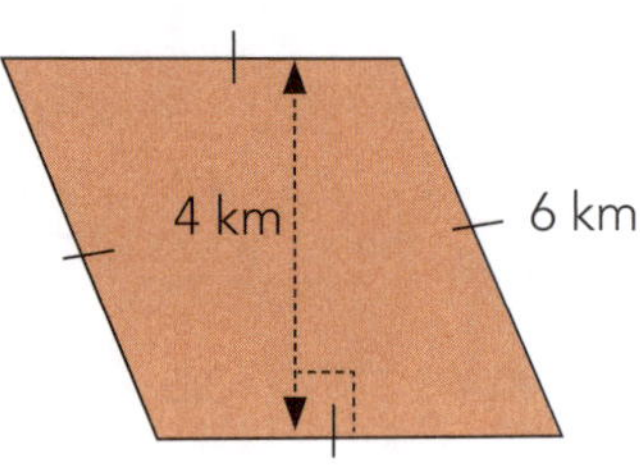

5

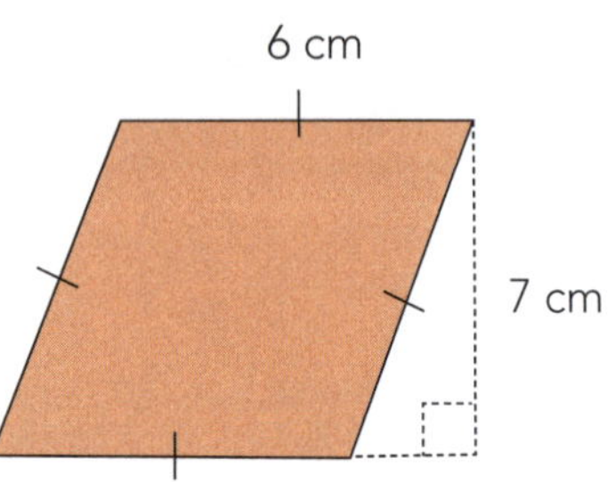

6

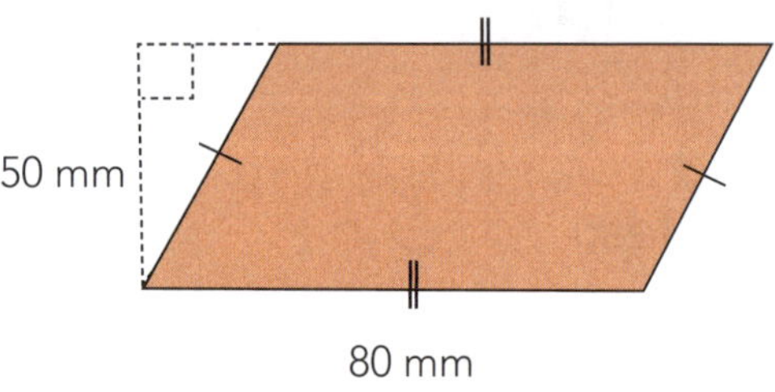

7

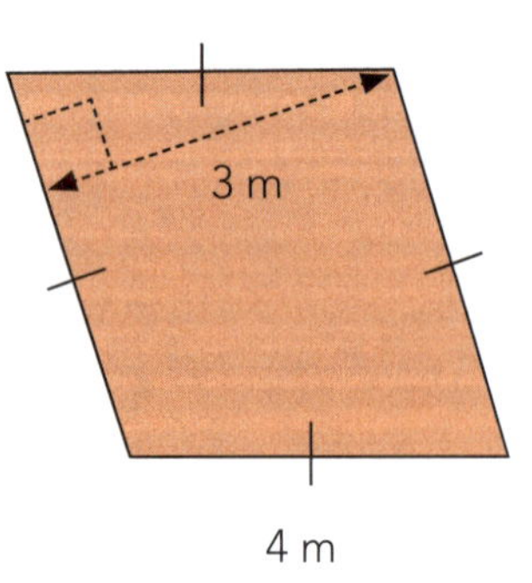

8

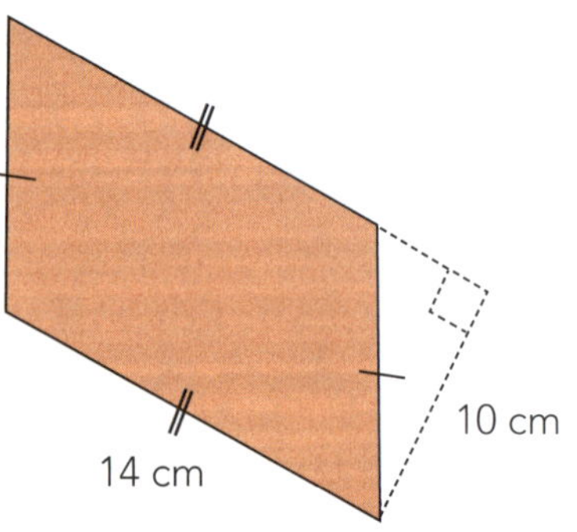

ISBN: 9780170447171

Triangles

- A **triangle** has three sides, and is half a rectangle or square.

$$\text{Area} = \frac{1}{2} \times \text{base} \times \text{vertical height}$$

$$A = \frac{1}{2} \times b \times h$$

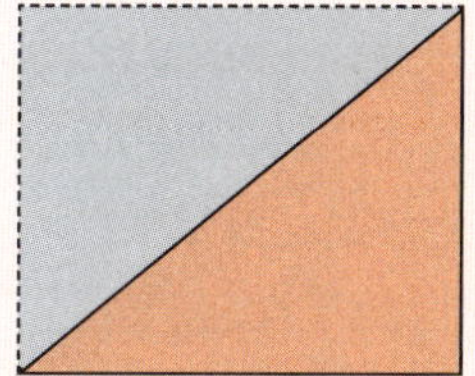

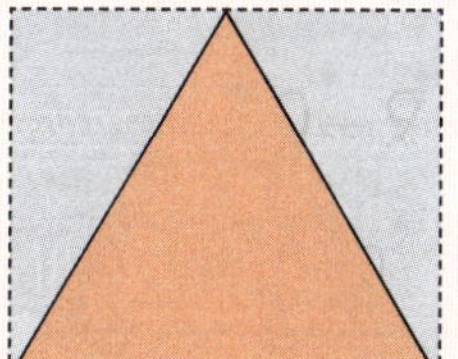

$$\text{Area} = \frac{1}{2} \times (\text{area rectangle}) = \frac{1}{2} \times \text{base} \times \text{height} = \frac{1}{2} \times b \times h$$

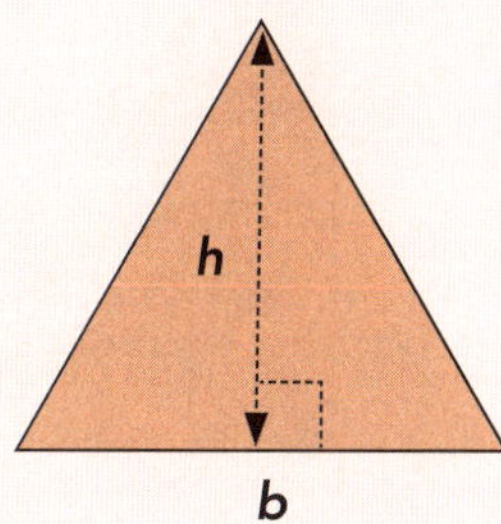

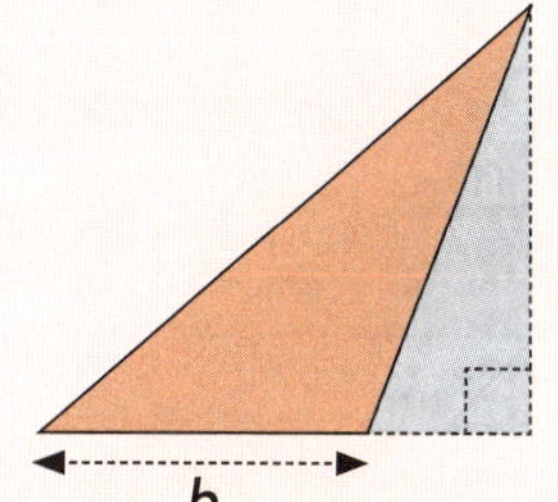

You must use the **vertical** height.

Examples:

1

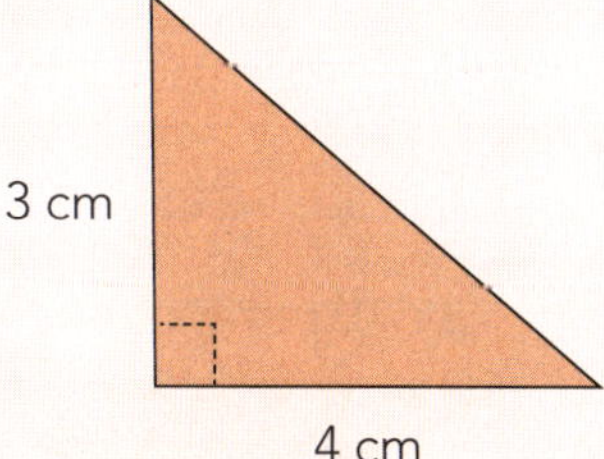

$$\text{Area} = \frac{1}{2} \times b \times h$$

$$= \frac{1}{2} \times 4 \times 3$$

$$= 6 \text{ cm}^2$$

2

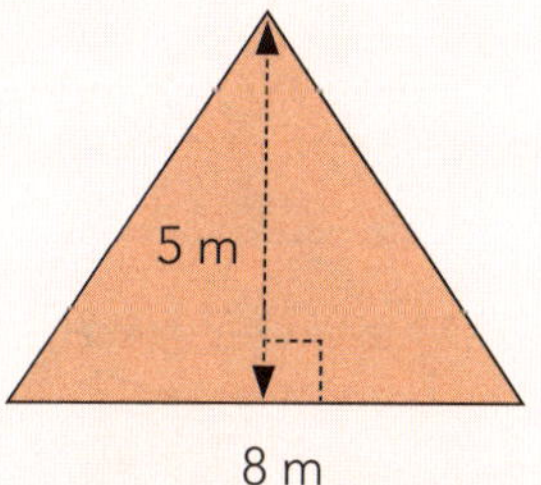

$$\text{Area} = \frac{1}{2} \times b \times h$$

$$= \frac{1}{2} \times 8 \times 5$$

$$= 20 \text{ m}^2$$

ISBN: 9780170447171

Calculate the areas of these shapes.

1

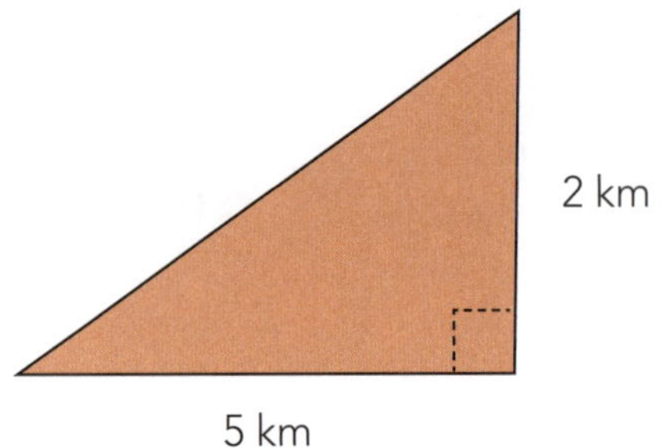

2

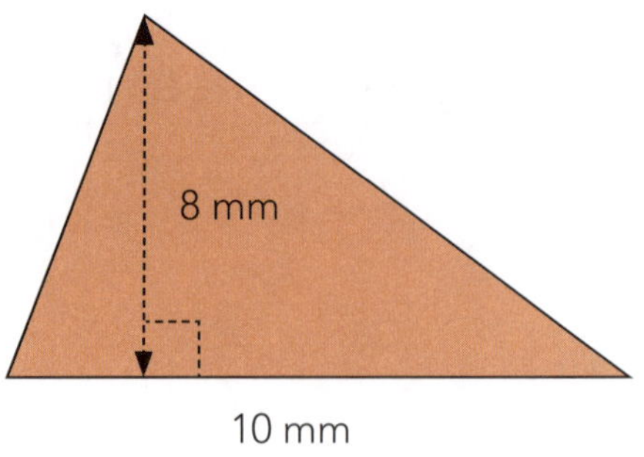

3

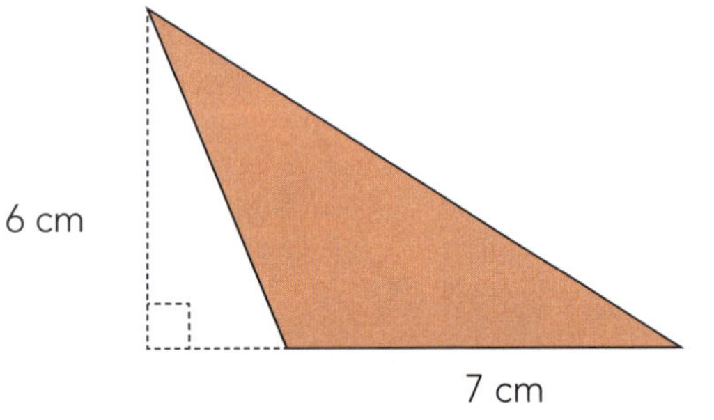

4

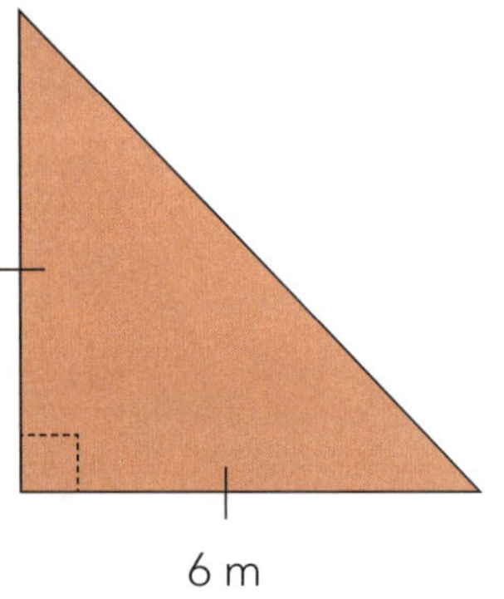

5

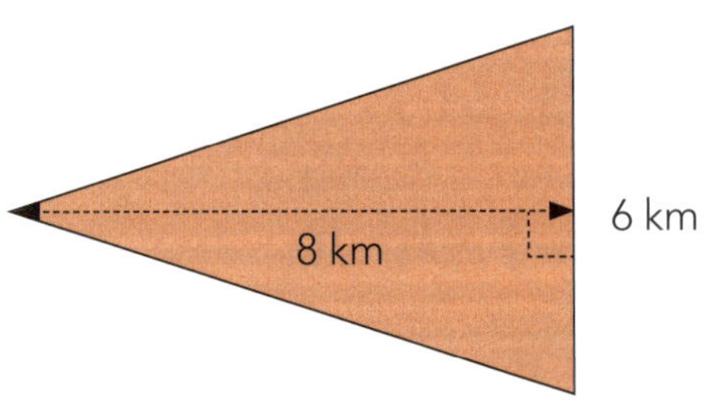

6

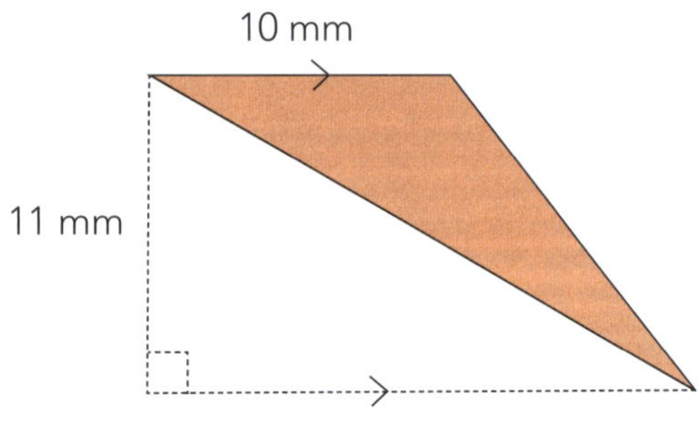

 ISBN: 9780170447171

Things to look out for

Extra measurements

- There may be measurements that are not needed for calculating the area.

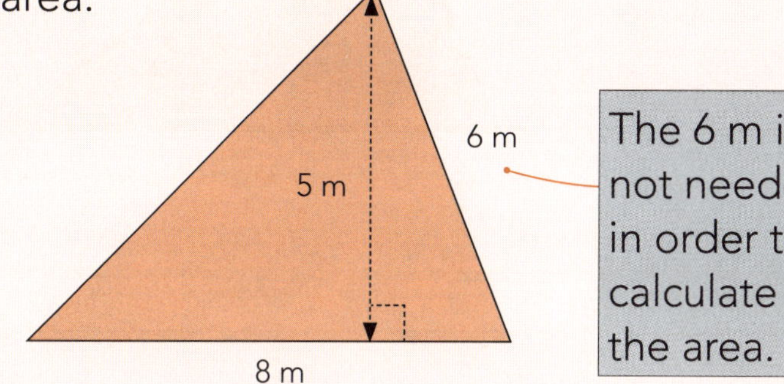

$$\text{Area} = \frac{1}{2} \times b \times h$$
$$= \frac{1}{2} \times 8 \times 5$$
$$= 20\text{ m}^2$$

Different units

- Some shapes may have measurements with different units.
- You need to make sure that all the information you need is in the same units before calculating the area.

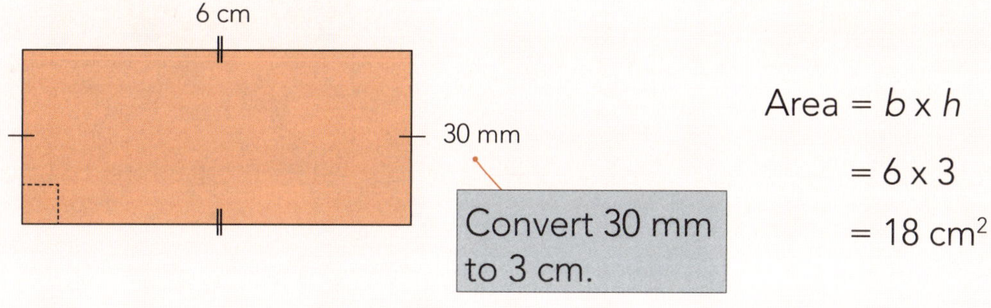

$$\text{Area} = b \times h$$
$$= 6 \times 3$$
$$= 18\text{ cm}^2$$

Calculate the areas of the following shapes.

1 Write your answer in square metres (m^2).

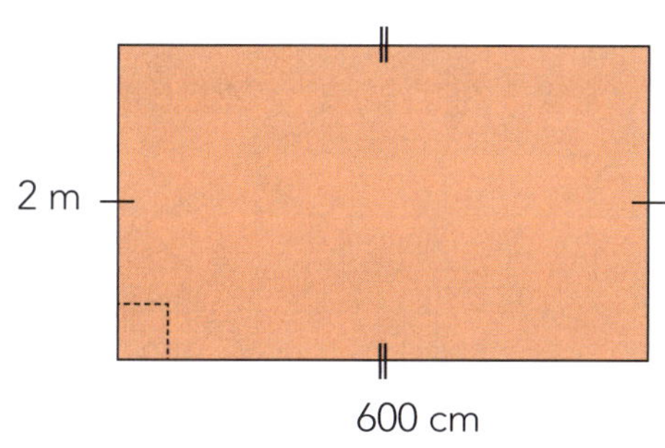

2

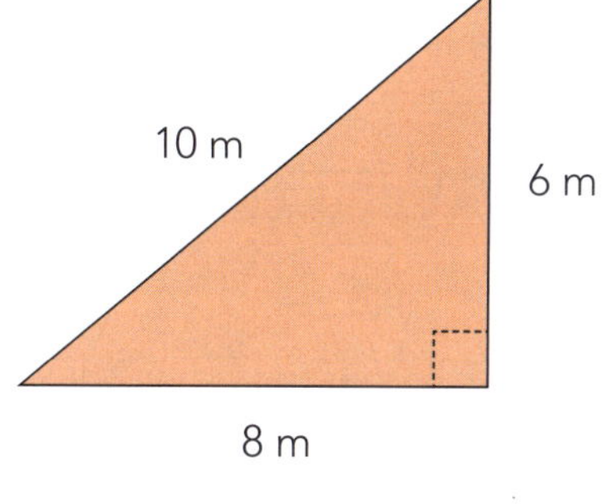

3

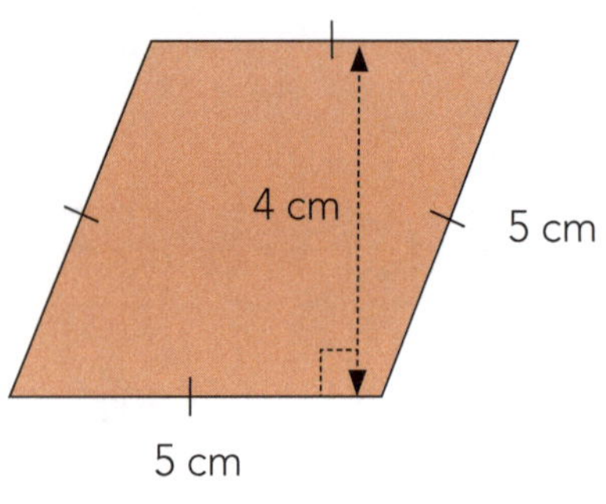

4 Write your answer in square centimetres (cm^2).

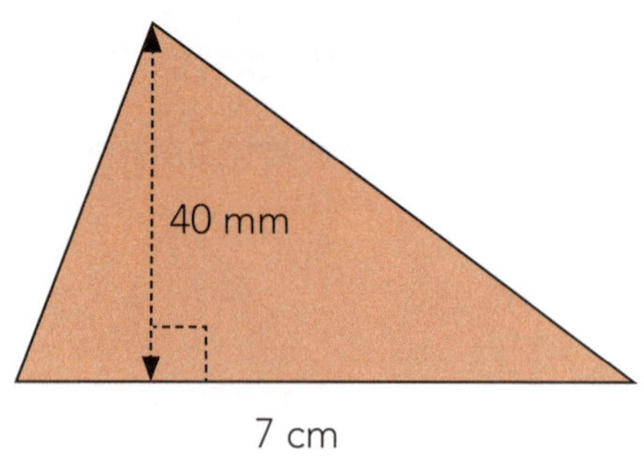

5

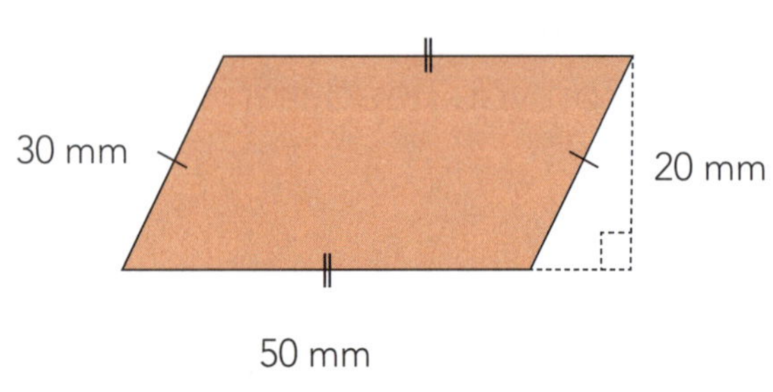

6 Write your answer in square kilometres (km^2).

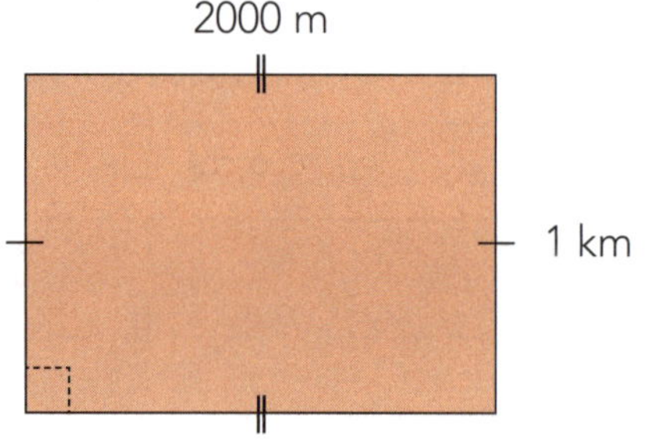

7 Write your answer in square metres (m^2).

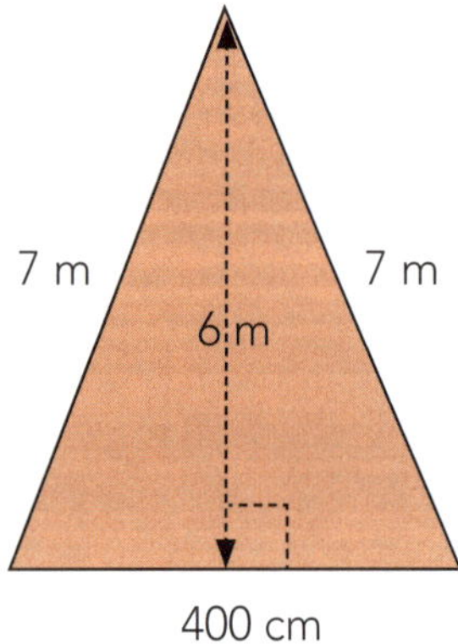

8 Write your answer in square metres (m^2).

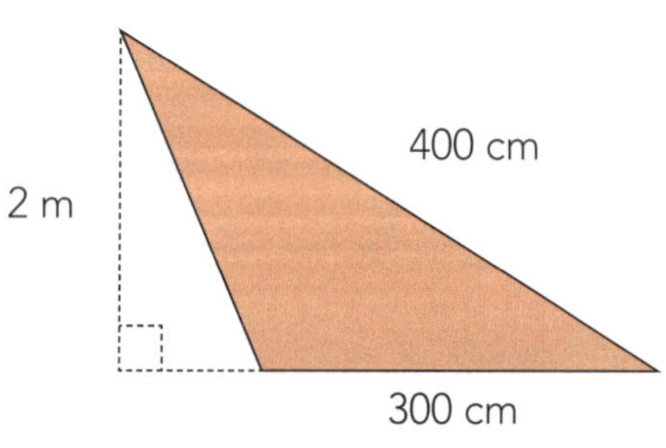

ISBN: 9780170447171

Working backwards

- At times, you maybe required to work 'backwards'.

Examples:

1 The area of this rectangle is 24 m^2.
Calculate its height.

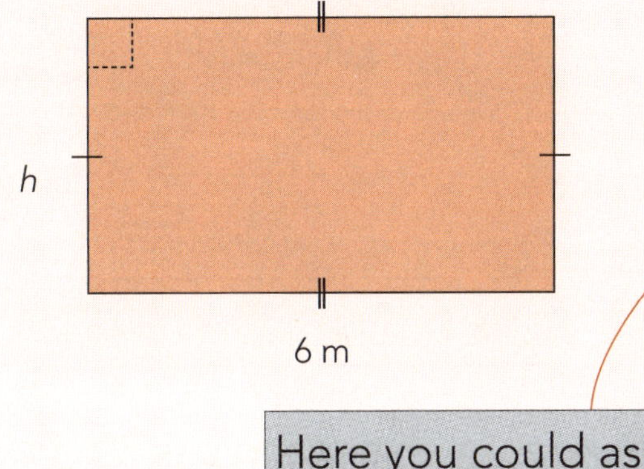

Step 1: Write the formula.

$$\text{Area} = b \times h$$

Step 2: Put the values in that you know.

$$24 = 6 \times h$$

Here you could ask yourself, 6 x ? = 24.

Step 3: Rearrange.

$$h = 24 \div 6$$

Step 4: Solve (don't forget units).

$$h = 4 \text{ m}$$

Step 5: Check that it works using the formula.

$$\text{Area} = b \times h$$
$$= 6 \times 4$$
$$= 24 \text{ m}^2$$

This is true, so we are correct!

2 The area of this triangle is 20 cm^2.
Calculate the length of the base.

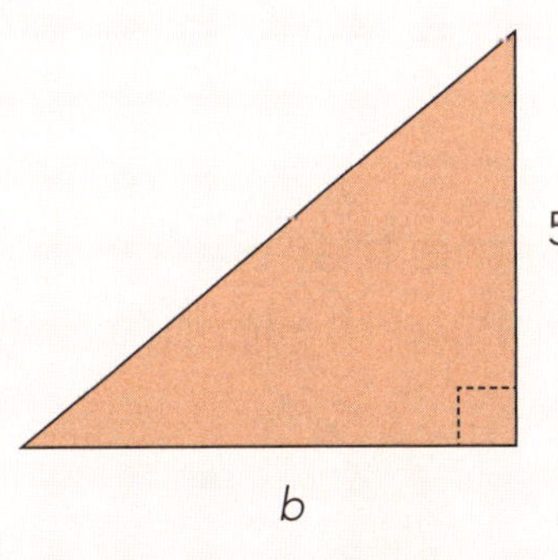

Step 1: Write the formula.

$$\text{Area} = \frac{1}{2} \times b \times h$$

Step 2: Put the values in that you know.

$$20 = \frac{1}{2} \times b \times 5$$

Here you could ask yourself, 5 x ? = 20, and then double the answer.

Step 3: Rearrange.

$$b = 20 \div 5 \div \frac{1}{2}$$

Step 4: Solve (don't forget units).

$$b = 8 \text{ cm}$$

Step 5: Check that it works using the formula.

$$\text{Area} = \frac{1}{2} \times b \times h$$
$$= \frac{1}{2} \times 8 \times 5$$
$$= 20 \text{ cm}^2$$

This is true, so we are correct! If it wasn't, then you would need to go back and check your working.

ISBN: 9780170447171

Answer the following questions.

1 The area of this rectangle is 18 cm^2. Calculate the length of its base, *b*.

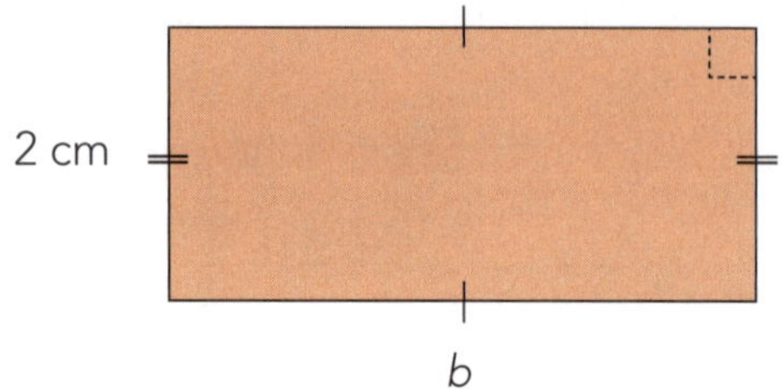

2 The area of this square is 25 m^2. Calculate the length of its sides.

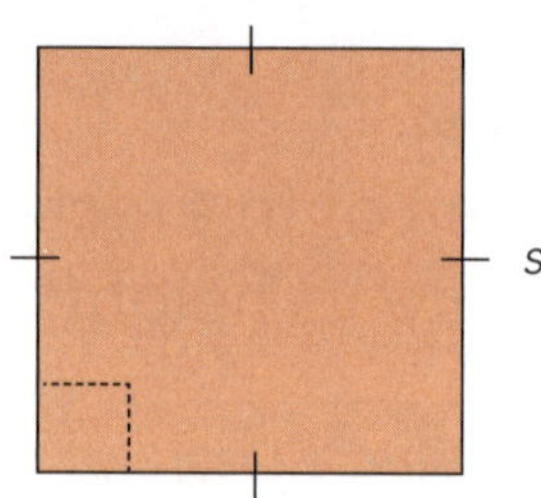

3 The area of this parallelogram is 45 km^2. Calculate its height, *h*.

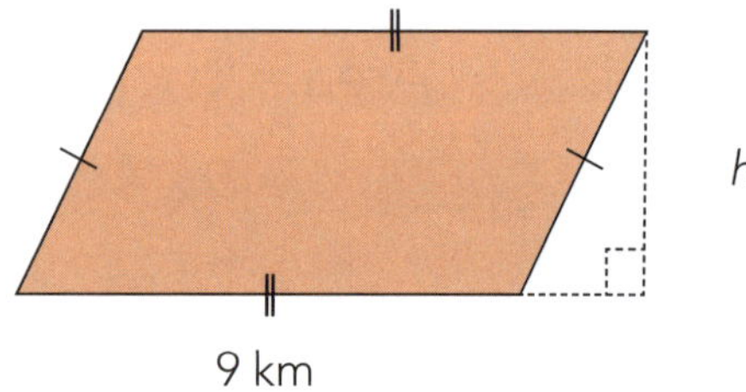

4 The area of this triangle is 30 cm^2. Calculate the length of side *h*.

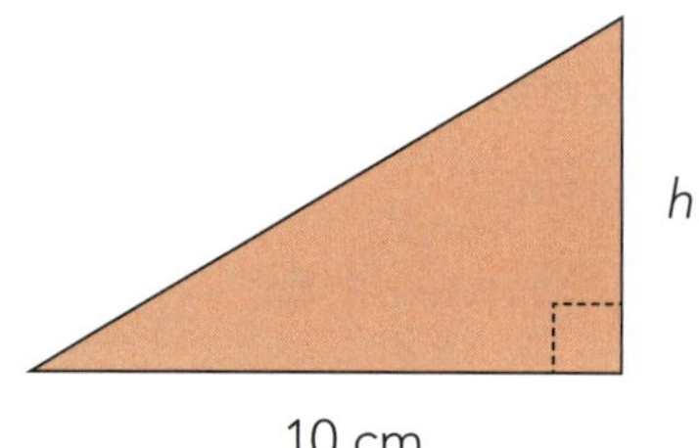

5 The area of this rhombus is 168 m^2. Calculate the length of its base, *b*.

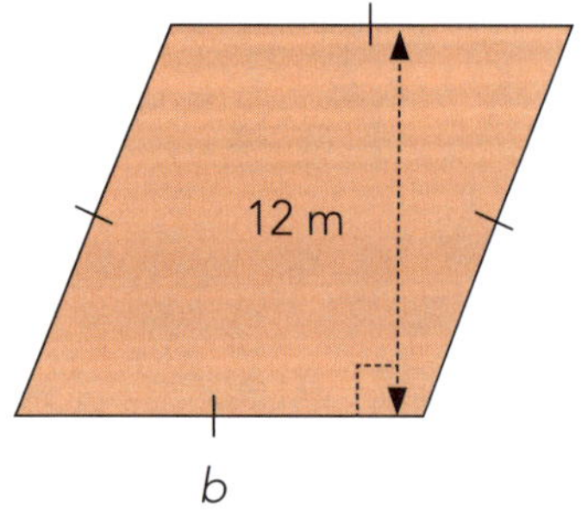

6 The area of this triangle is 27 m^2. Calculate the length of its base, *b*.

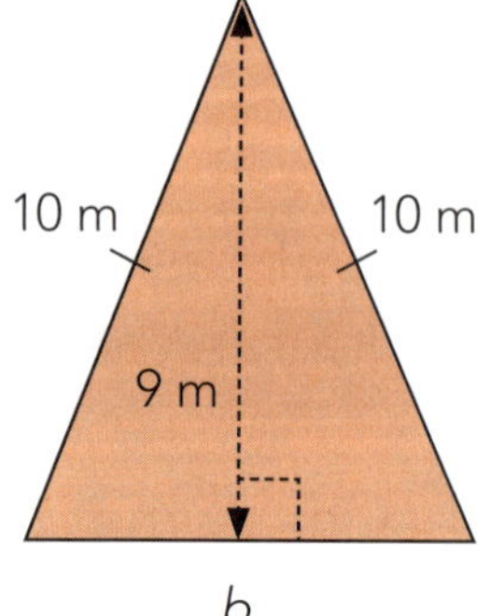

ISBN: 9780170447171

Compound shapes

- Remember, compound shapes are shapes that are made up of **other simple shapes**.
- You need to find the areas of the simple shapes and then **add** them together.

Examples:

1

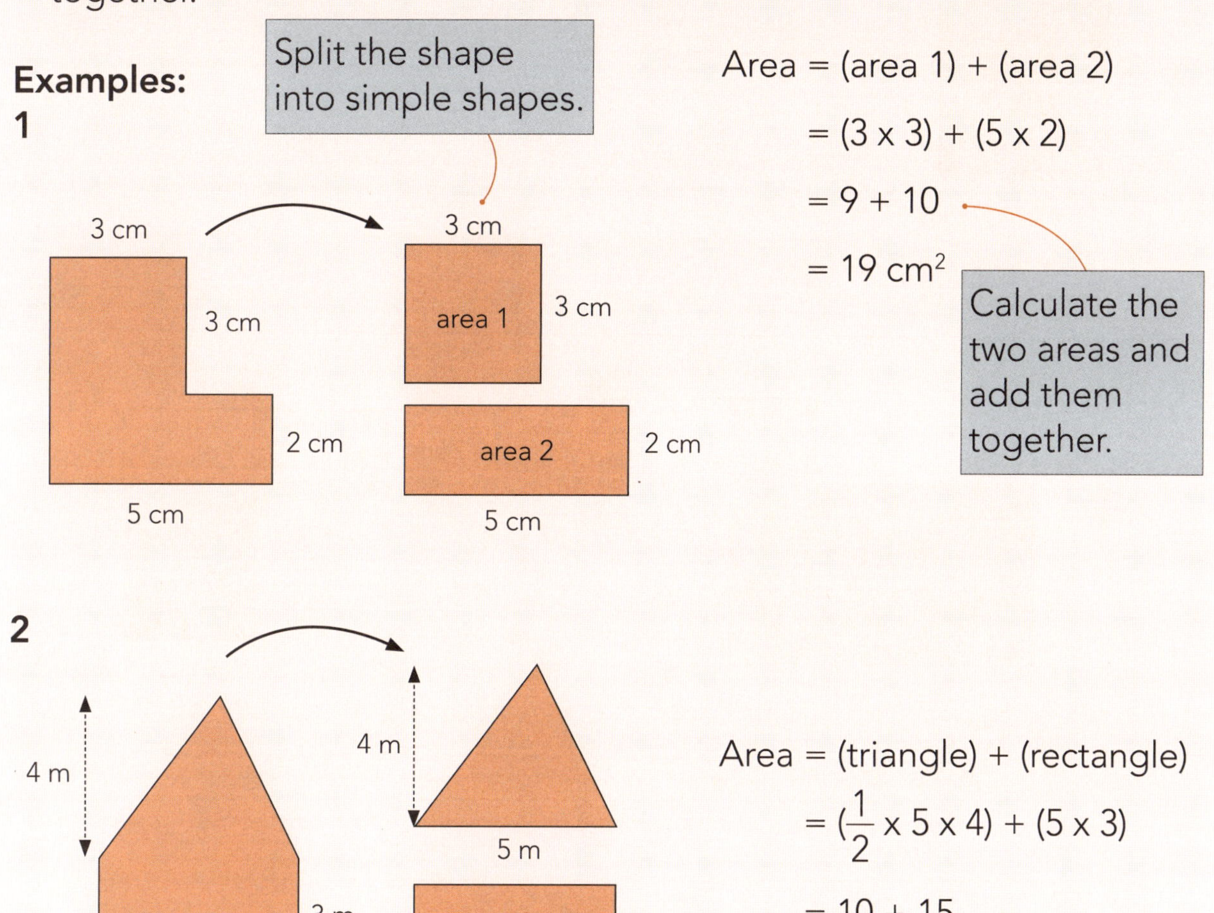

Area = (area 1) + (area 2)

$= (3 \times 3) + (5 \times 2)$

$= 9 + 10$

$= 19\ \text{cm}^2$

Area = (triangle) + (rectangle)

$= (\frac{1}{2} \times 5 \times 4) + (5 \times 3)$

$= 10 + 15$

$= 25\ \text{m}^2$

Calculate the areas of these shapes. All are made up of rectangles and triangles.

1

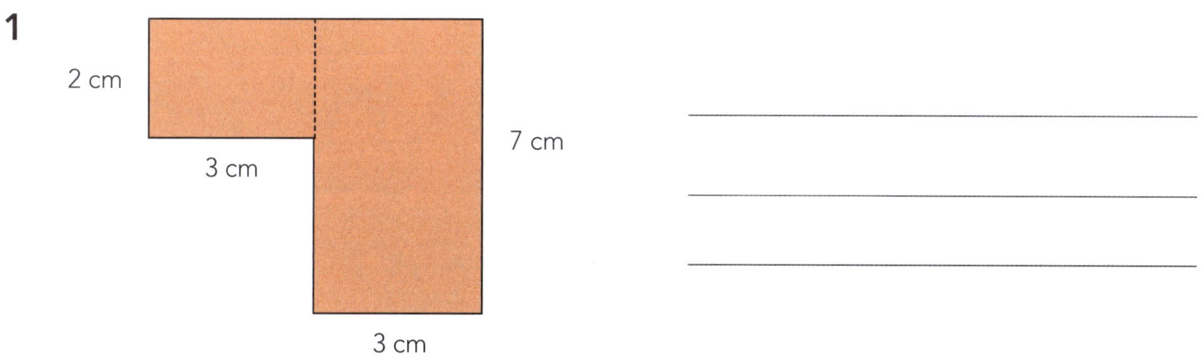

2

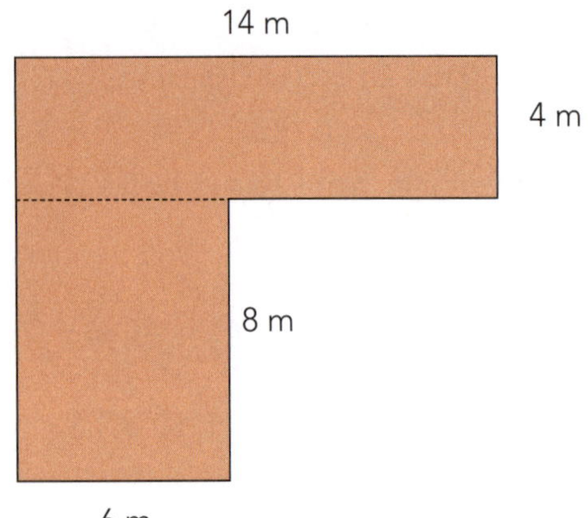

3

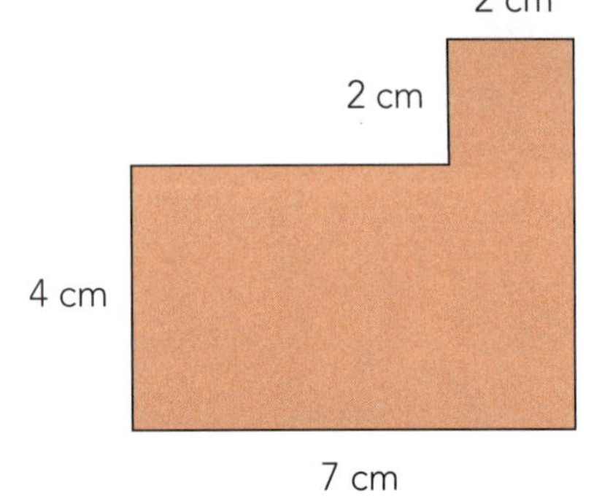

4

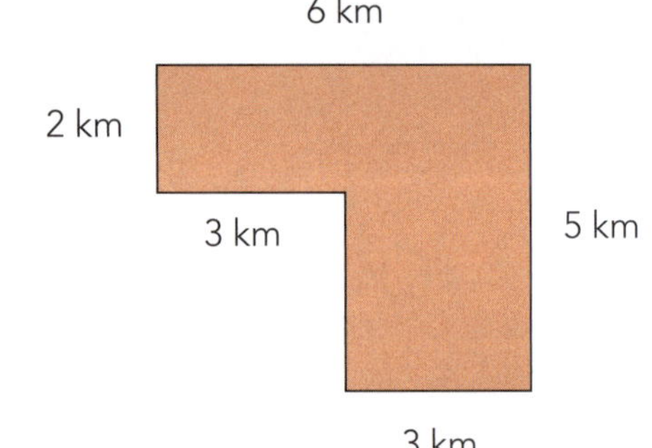

5

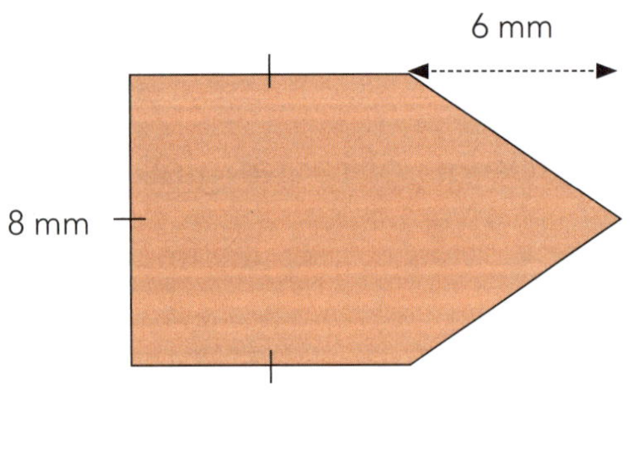

6

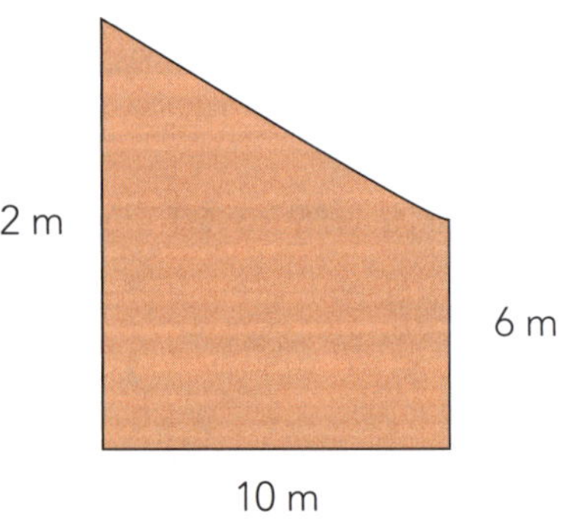

ISBN: 9780170447171

Shapes with holes

- You need to find the areas of the simple shapes and then **subtract** one from the other.

Example:

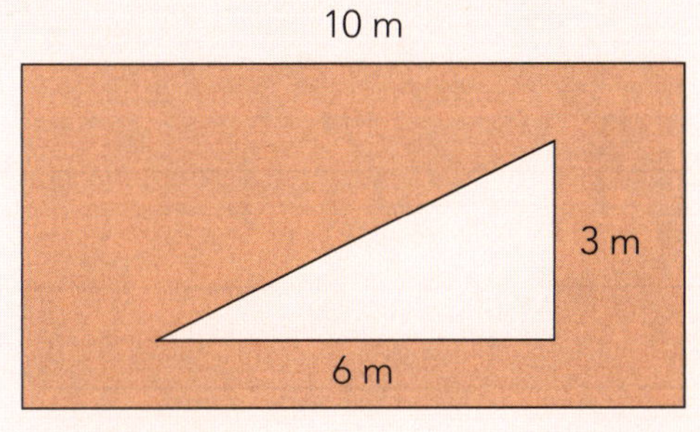

Shaded area = (rectangle) – (triangle)

$= (10 \times 5) - (\frac{1}{2} \times 6 \times 3)$

$= 50 - 9$

$= 41\ m^2$

Calculate the two areas and subtract one from the other.

Calculate the shaded areas of these shapes. All are made up of rectangles and triangles.

1

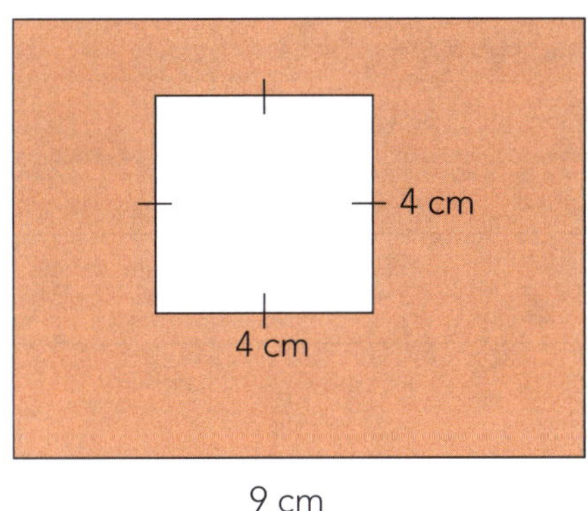

____

____

____

2

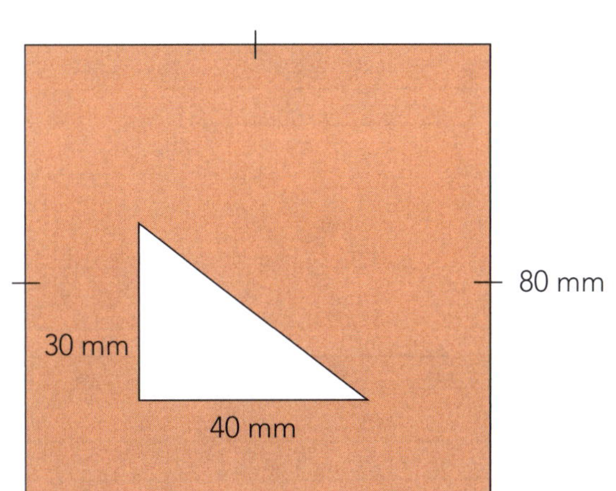

____

____

____

3

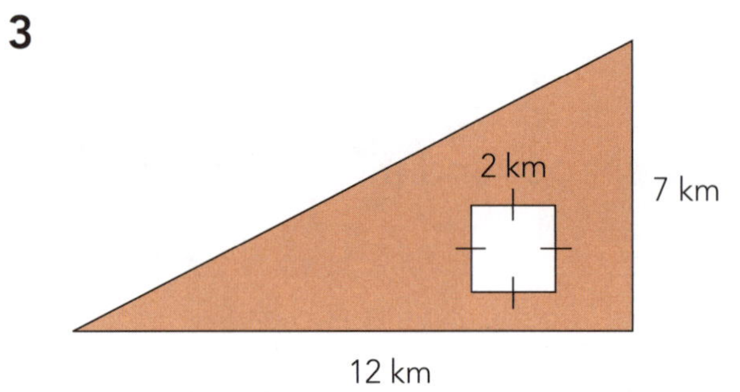

4

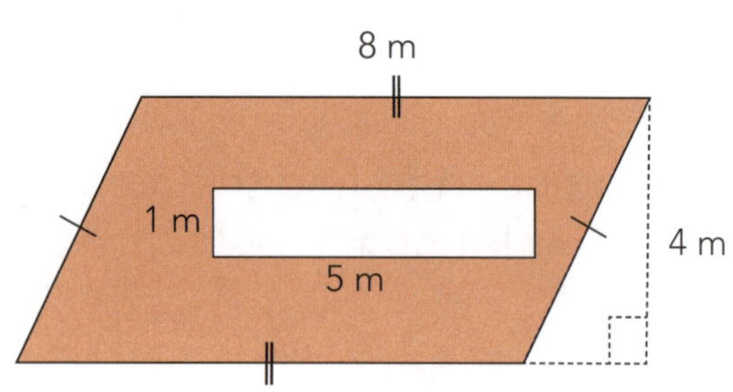

5

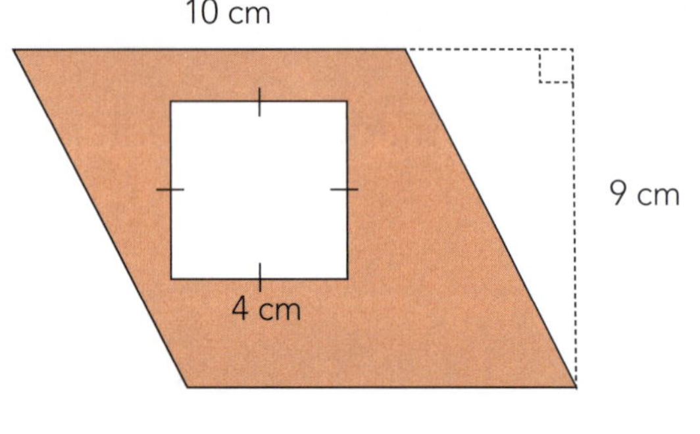

6

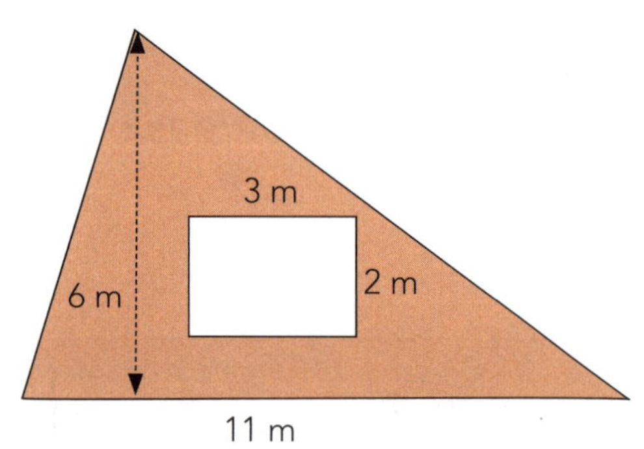

7

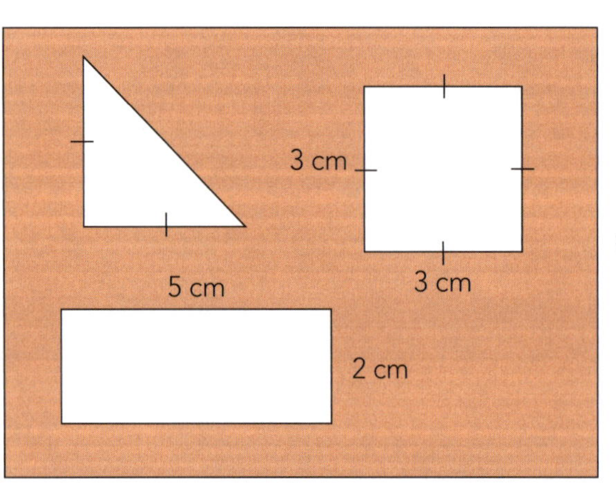

 ISBN: 9780170447171

Word questions

Answer the following questions. Don't forget to sketch a diagram first.

1 A rectangular bedroom measures 1.5 m by 2.1 m. What is the area of the bedroom?

____

____

2 Robert is planting a triangular garden bed. If the height is 2 m and the base is 3 m, what is the area of the garden bed?

____

____

3 The dimensions of a basketball court are 28 m by 15 m. What is the area of the court?

____

____

4 Bert is painting a triangular sign that is 45 cm at the base and has a height of 60 cm. If he is painting both sides, what area is he painting?

____

____

5 A roll of wrapping paper states that it is 50 m long and 750 mm wide. What is the area of the entire roll?

____

____

6 A ruler is 30 cm long and has an area of 120 cm^2. How wide is the ruler?

____

____

ISBN: 9780170447171

Challenge 2

Find the areas of these compound shapes. All are made up of rectanges and triangles.

1

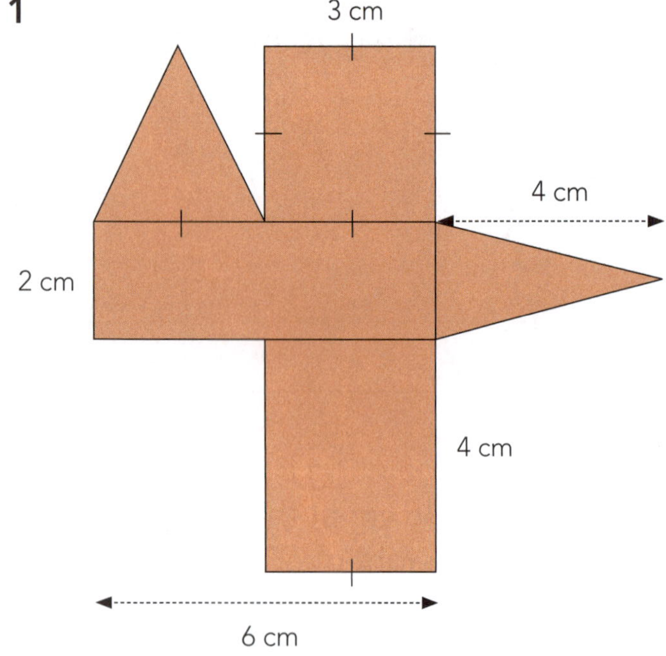

2

7 m

3 m

1 m

4 m

4 m

2 m

5 m

 ISBN: 9780170447171

Volume

Cuboids with cube blocks

If you can **fill** it, it's volume.

- The volume of a three-dimensional (3D) shape is the amount of **space** the shape occupies.
- A **cuboid** is a box shape, e.g. a shoebox.
- A **cube** is a box shape where all the dimensions are equal, e.g. a die.
- Each block represents 1 cm^3.

Volume = height x width x depth

$V = h \times w \times d$

Example:

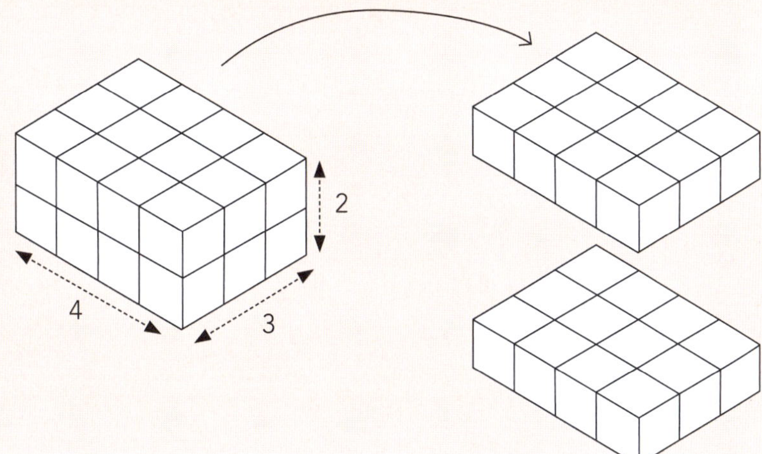

Volume = number of layers x number of blocks in one layer

= 2 x 4 x 3

= 24 cm^3

This is the same as **height x width x depth**.

When calculating volume, the units must be cubed (^{3}).

Calculate the volumes of these cuboids.

1

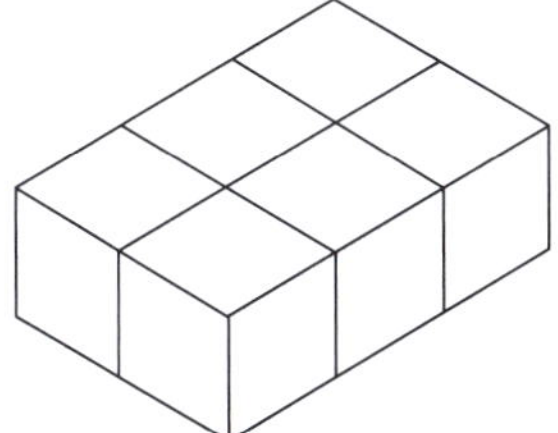

Volume = $h \times w \times d$

= ________________

= ________________

2

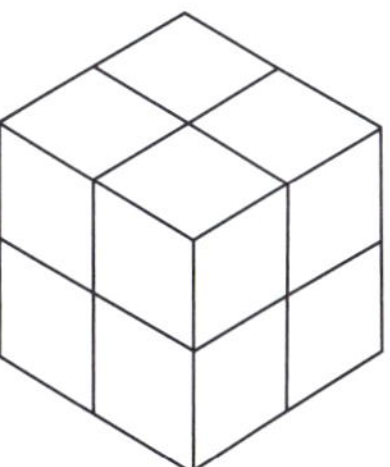

Volume = $h \times w \times d$

= ________________

= ________________

3

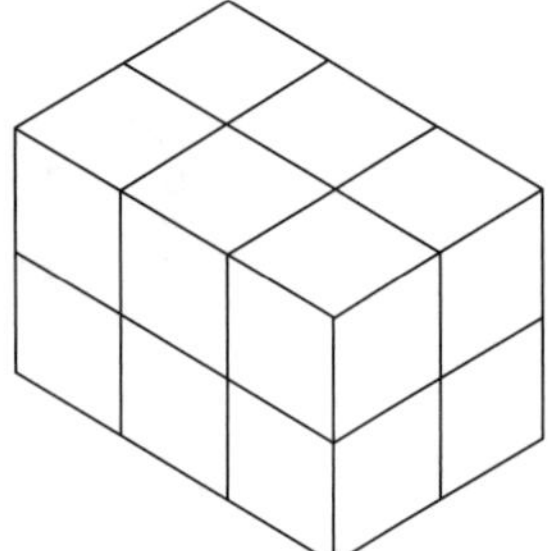

4

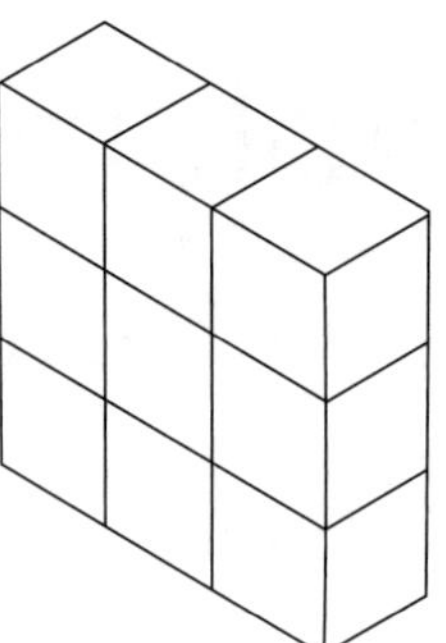

5

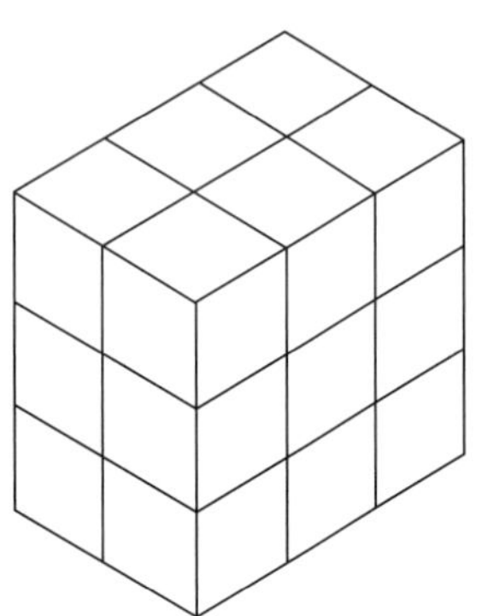

6

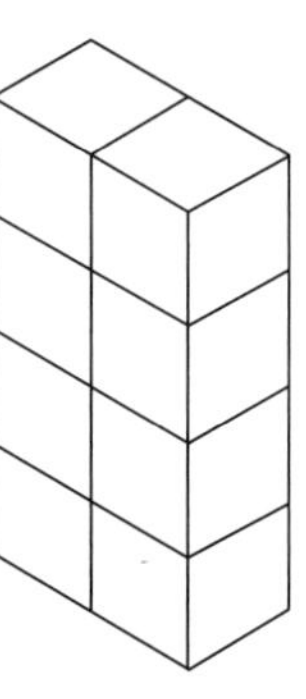

7

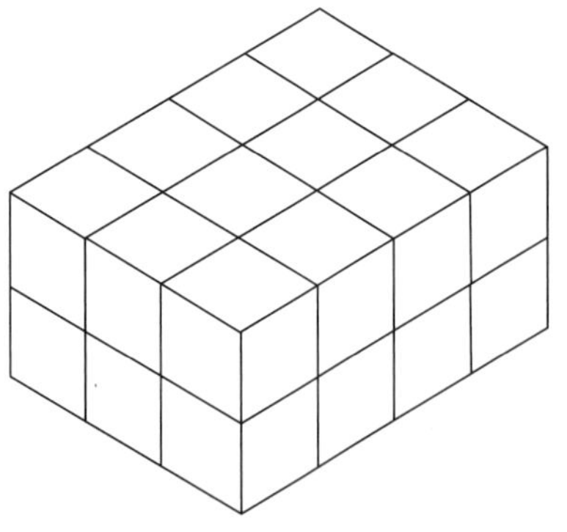

8

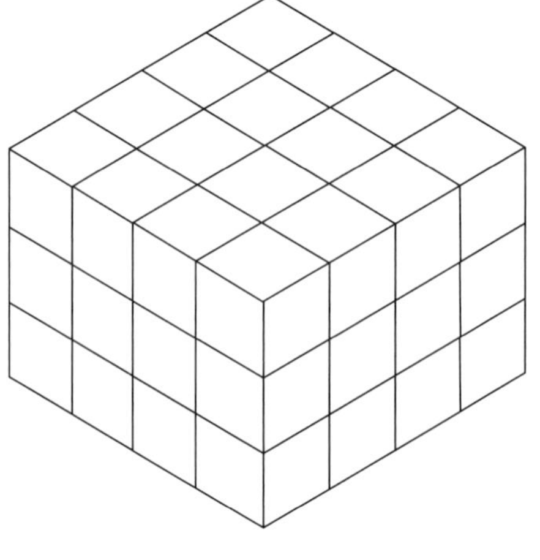

 ISBN: 9780170447171

Cuboids using the formula

- Remember, a **cuboid** is a box shape.

Volume = height x width x depth

V* = *h* x *w* x *d

Examples:

1

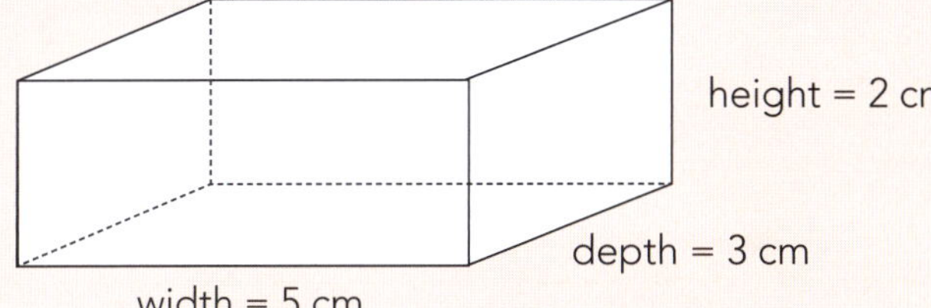

Volume = $h \times w \times d$
= 2 x 5 x 3
= 30 cm^3

2 Another way to think about it is to find the area of the 'face' and multiply it by the depth.

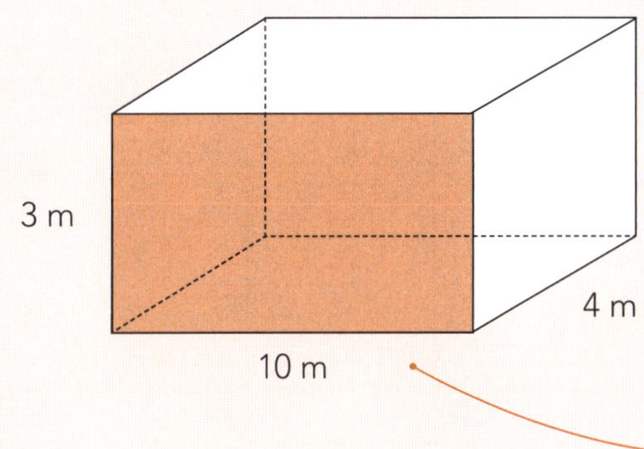

Volume = **area of face** x d
= **(3 x 10)** x 4
= **(30)** x 4
= 120 m^3

Area of the face is **30 m^2**, which is multiplied by the depth (4 m).

Calculate the volumes of these cuboids.

1

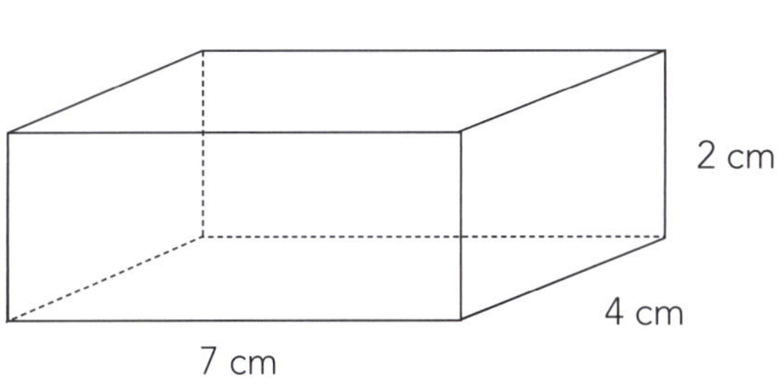

____

____

2

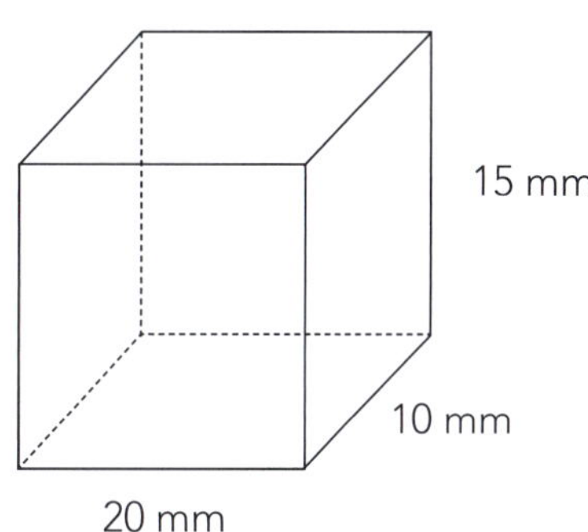

____

____

ISBN: 9780170447171

3

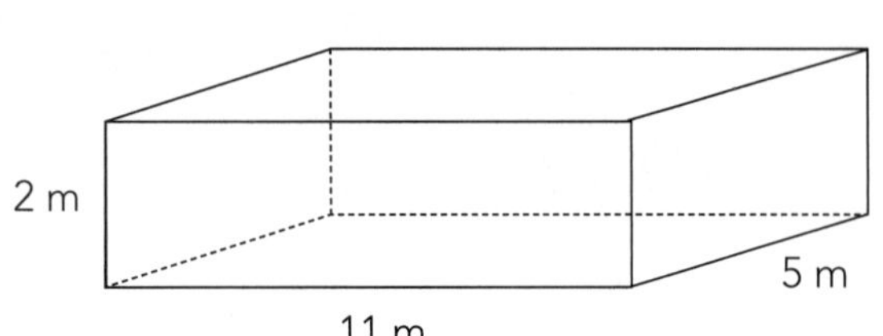

4

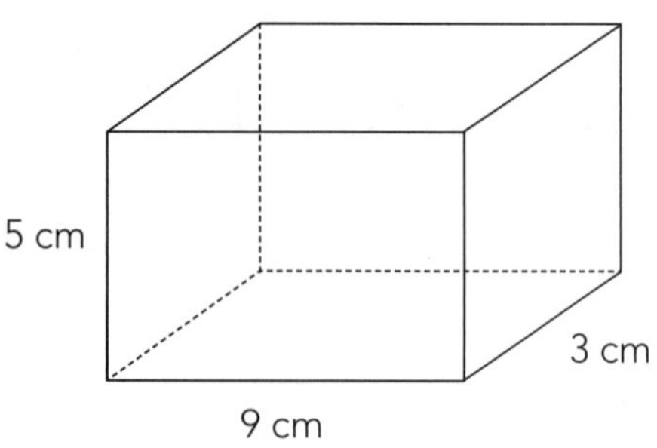

5

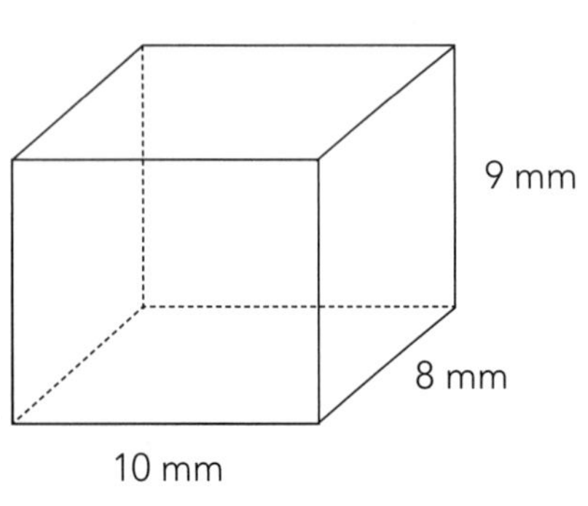

6

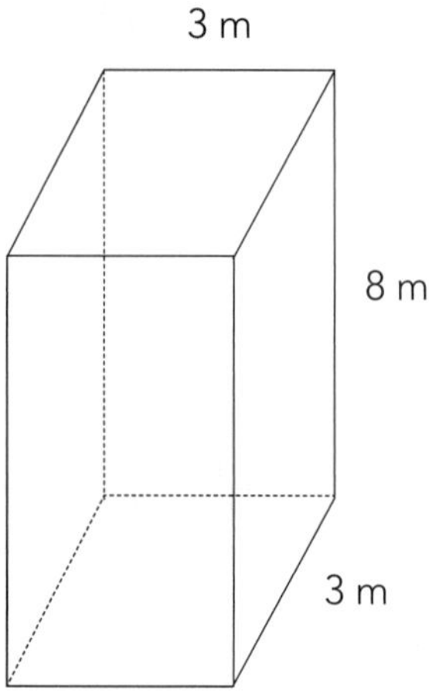

7

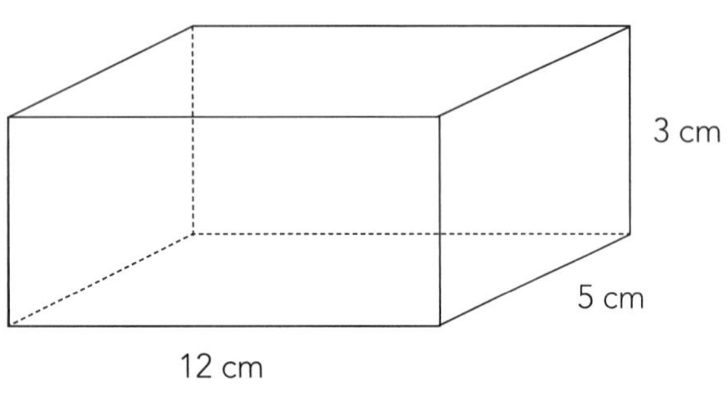

8 This is a cube.

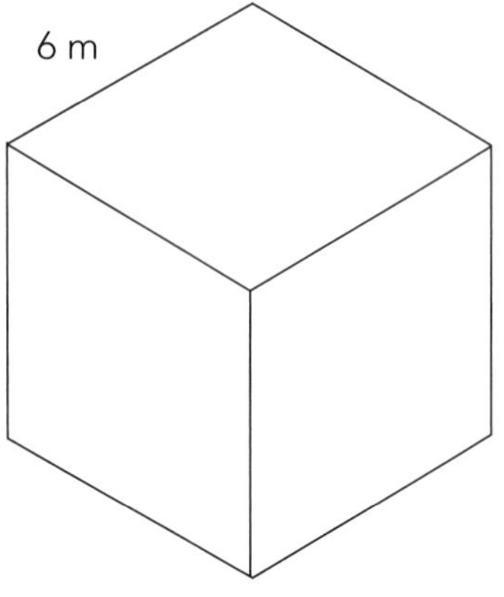

 ISBN: 9780170447171

Things to look out for

Different units

- Some shapes may have measurements with different units.
- You need to make sure that all the information you need is in the same units before calculating the volume.

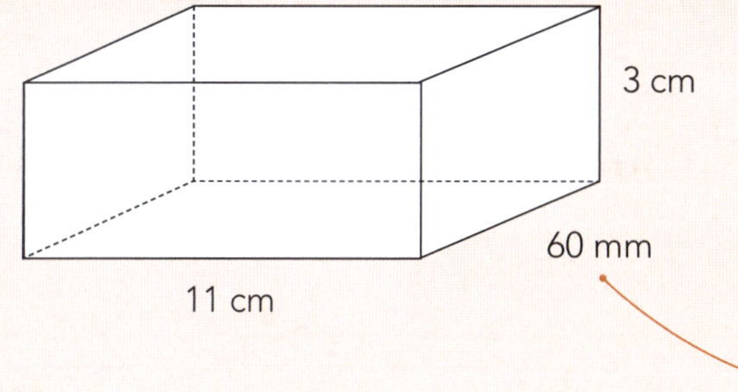

Volume = $h \times w \times d$

$= 3 \times 11 \times 6$

$= 198\ \text{cm}^3$

Convert 60 mm to 6 cm.

Calculate the volumes of the following shapes.

1 Write your answer in cubic centimetres (cm^3).

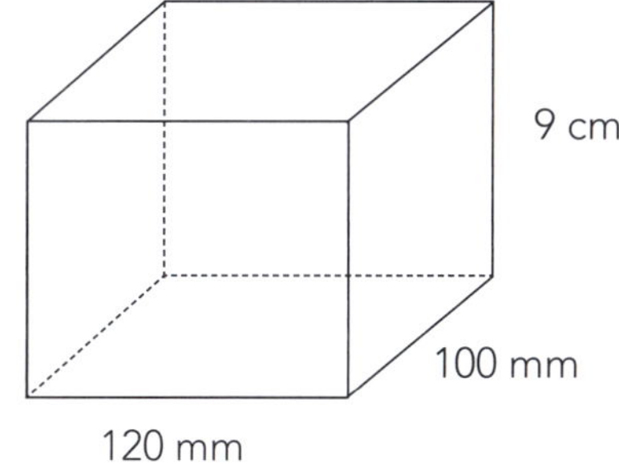

2 Write your answer in cubic metres (m^3).

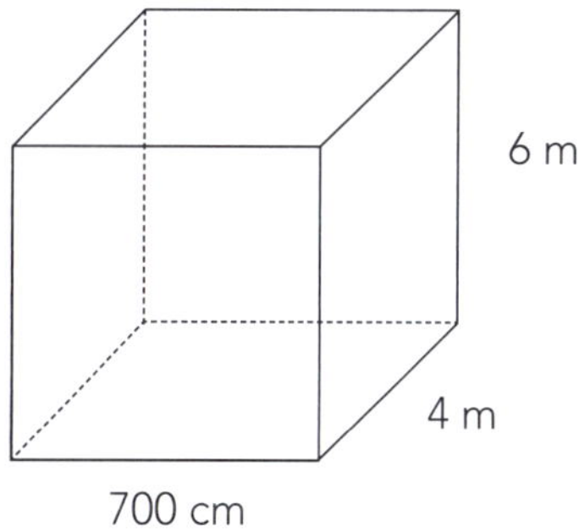

3 Write your answer in cubic centimetres (cm^3).

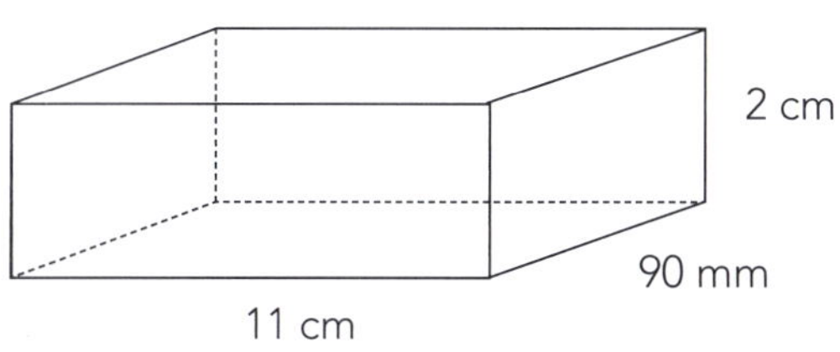

4 Write your answer in cubic metres (m^3).

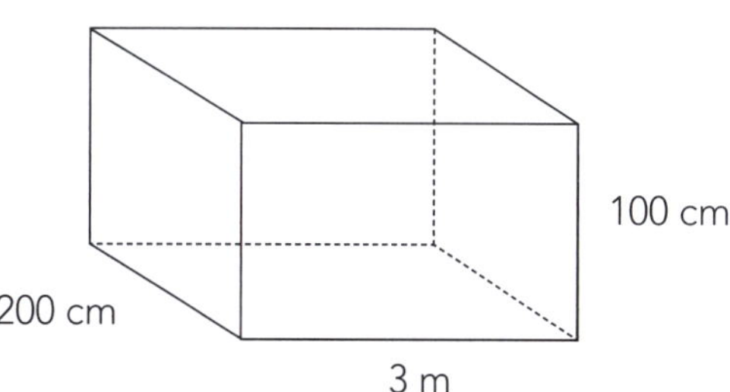

ISBN: 9780170447171

Working backwards

- At times, you maybe required to work 'backwards'.

Example:

The volume of this cuboid is 150 m^3. Calculate its height.

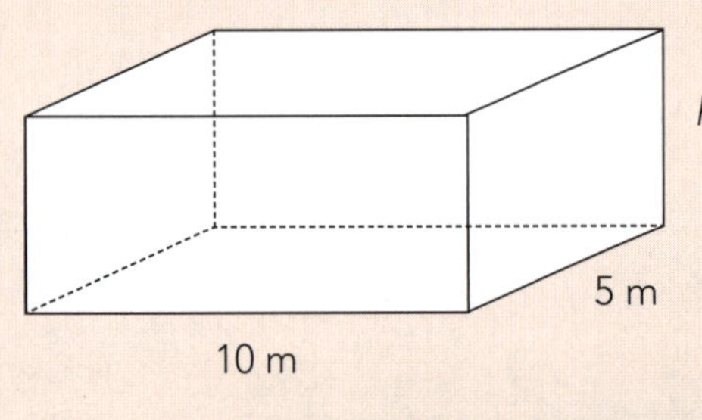

Step 1: Write the formula.

Volume = $h \times w \times d$

Step 2: Put the values in that you know.

$150 = h \times 10 \times 5$

Here you could ask yourself, $50 \times ? = 150$.

Step 3: Rearrange.

$h = 150 \div 10 \div 5$

Step 4: Solve (don't forget units).

$h = 3$ m

Step 5: Check that it works using the formula.

Volume = $h \times w \times d$

$= 3 \times 10 \times 5$

$= 150$ m^3

This is true, so we are correct!

Answer the following questions.

1 The volume of this cuboid is 60 cm^3. Calculate the depth.

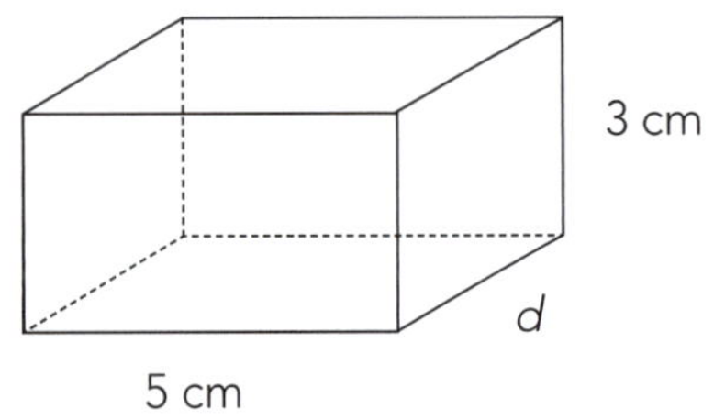

2 The volume of this cuboid is 48 m^3. Calculate the width.

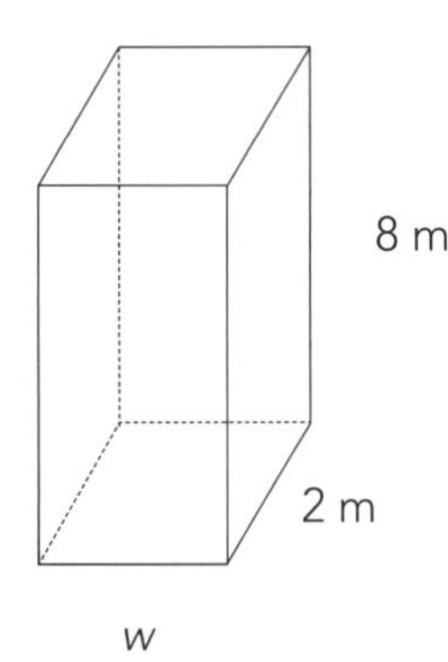

3 The volume of this cube is 343 cm^3. Calculate the lengths of the sides.

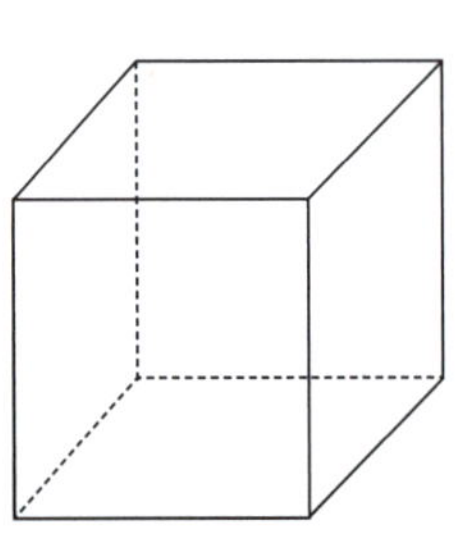

 ISBN: 9780170447171

Mixing it up

1 Calculate the volume of this cuboid in cubic metres (m^3).

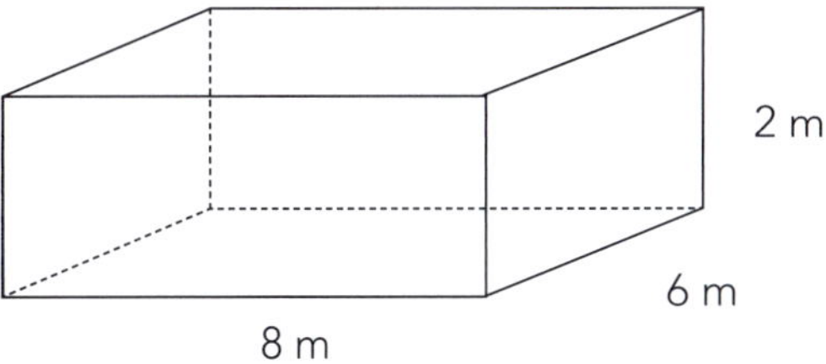

2 The volume of this cuboid is 180 cm^3. Calculate its height, *h*.

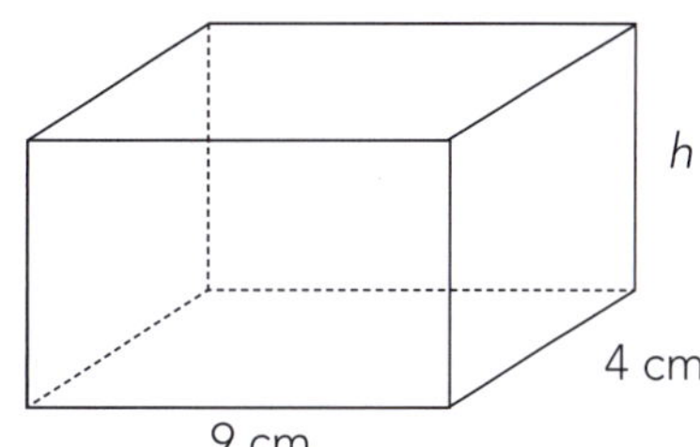

3 The volume of this cuboid is 70 m^3. Calculate its depth, *d*.

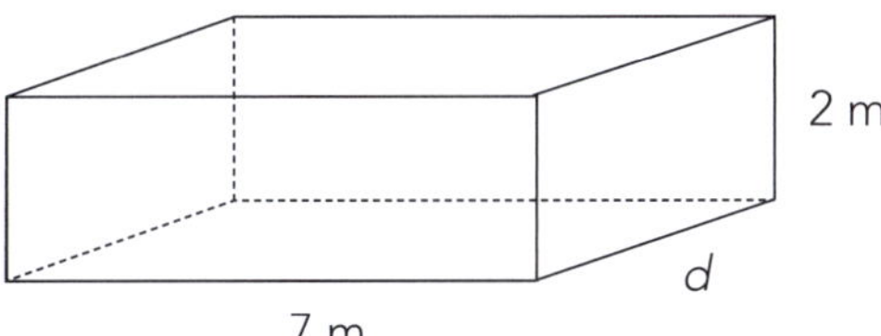

4 Calculate the volume of this cuboid in cubic centimetres (cm^3).

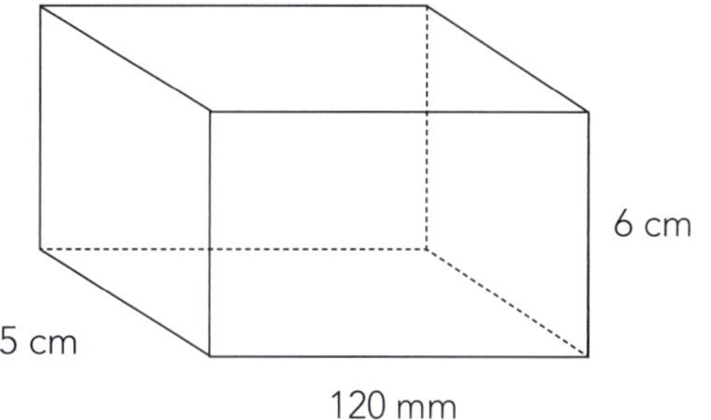

5 Calculate the volume of this cuboid in cubic metres (m^3).

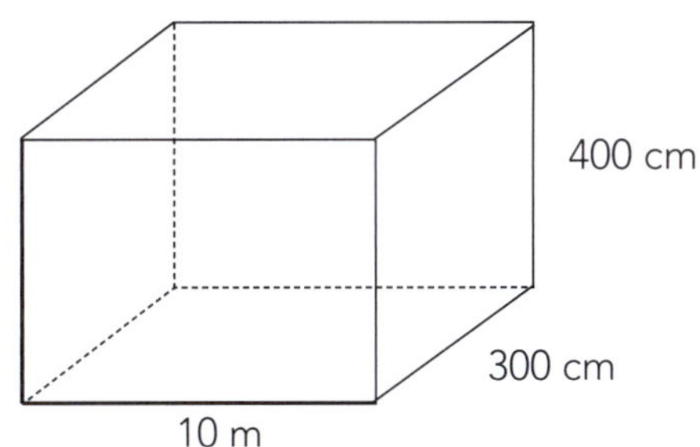

6 The volume of this cuboid is 105 m^3. Calculate its width, *w*, in metres (cm).

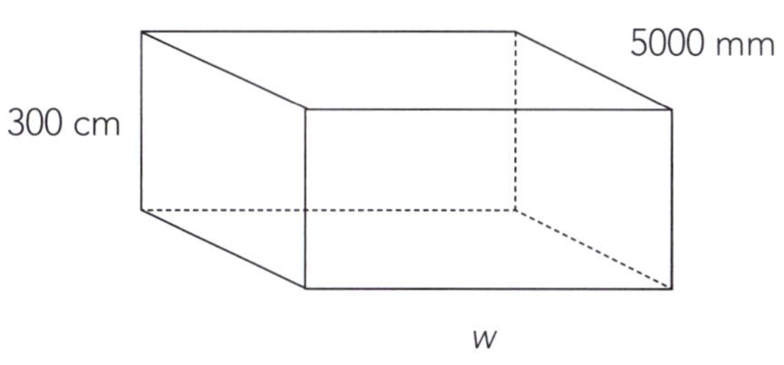

ISBN: 9780170447171

Revision 1

1 Write the abbreviations for these units.

a centimetre ____________ b second ____________

c gram ____________ d millilitre ____________

2 Write the meaning of these abbreviations.

a tbsp ____________ b km ____________

c mm ____________ d L ____________

3 Convert these measurements.

a 2 min = ____________ s b 90 mm = ____________ cm

c 9 g = ____________ mg d 5 L = ____________ mL

e 3 m = ____________ cm f 4 h = ____________ min

g 4 km = ____________ m h 3000 mg = ____________ g

i 48 h = ____________ d j 500 cm = ____________ m

4 Convert these times into digital time.

a Quarter past nine: b Ten to four:

____________ a.m. ____________ p.m.

c d

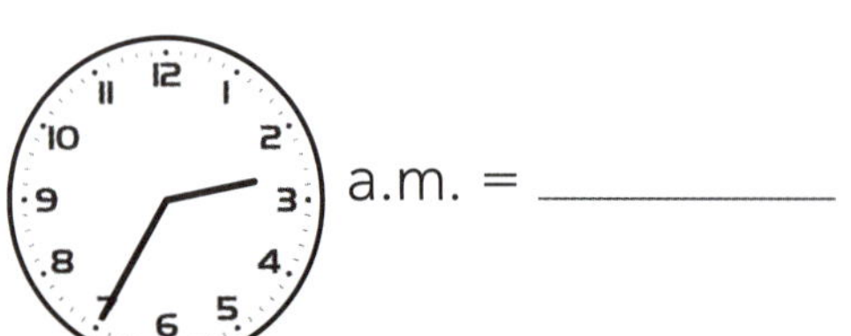

a.m. = ____________ p.m. = ____________

 ISBN: 9780170447171

5 Convert these times to 12-hour times.

a 06:14 = ______________ b 21:09 = ______________

6 Convert these times to 24-hour times.

a 9.51 a.m. = ______________ b 3.15 p.m. = ______________

c Half past eight p.m. = ______________ d Five to ten p.m. = ______________

7 Circle or highlight the most likely unit of measurement for these items.

a The amount of time it takes to eat dinner.

d L km min

b The length of your house key.

t km mm mL

c The mass of a brick.

tsp kg cm t

d The amount of juice in a drink bottle.

s m mL tbsp

8 Write the measurements given by the pointers or scales.

A = __________ B = __________ C = __________

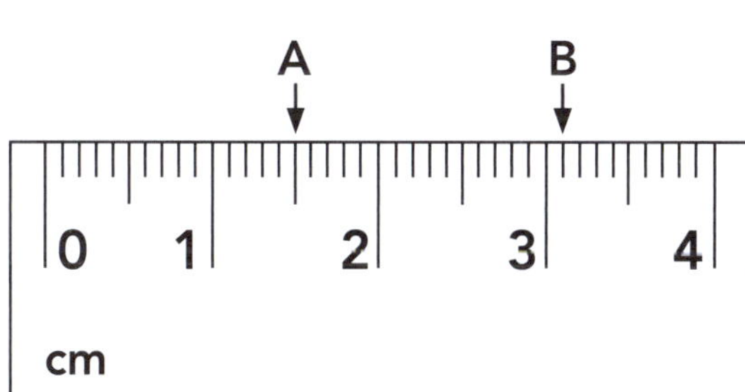

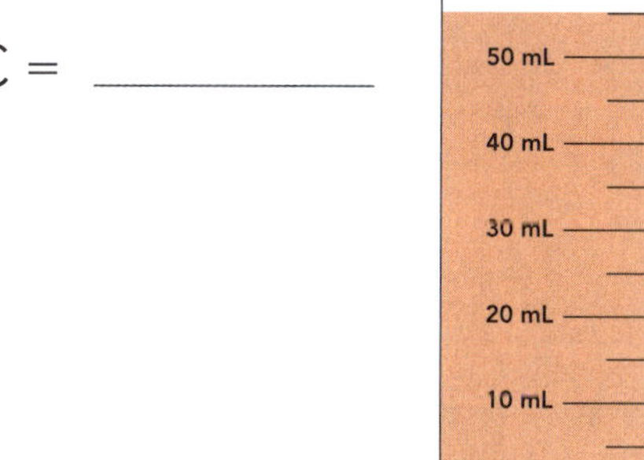

9 Colour the diagrams to show these measurements.

a 70 mL

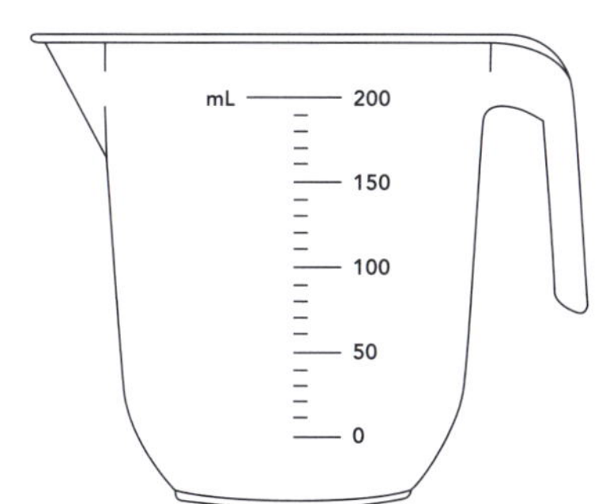

b 35°C

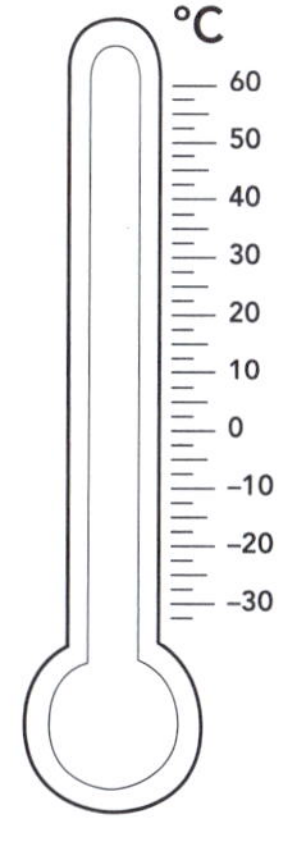

ISBN: 9780170447171

10 Calculate the perimeters of these shapes.

a

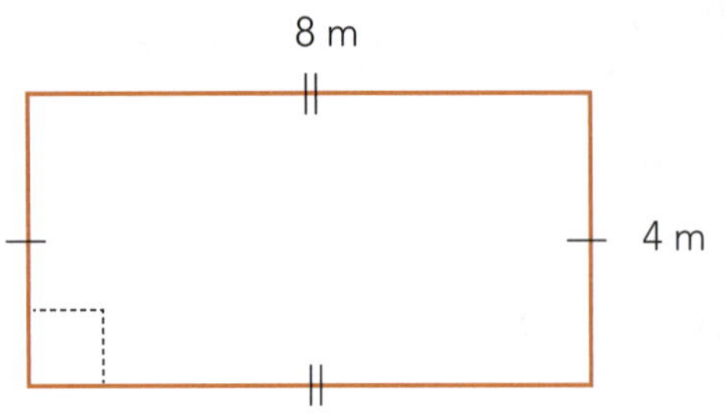

b

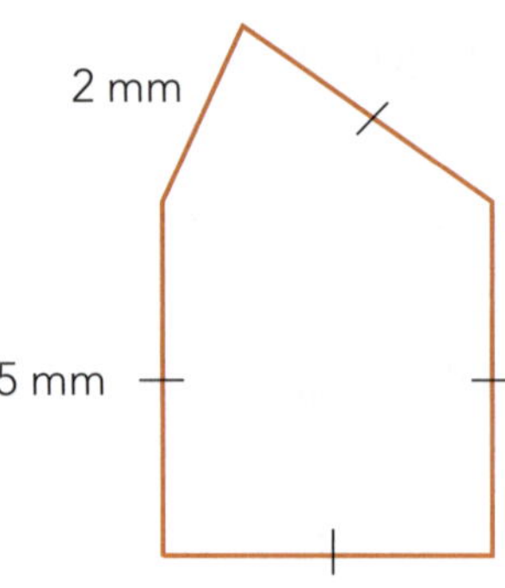

11 Calculate the shaded areas of these shapes.

a

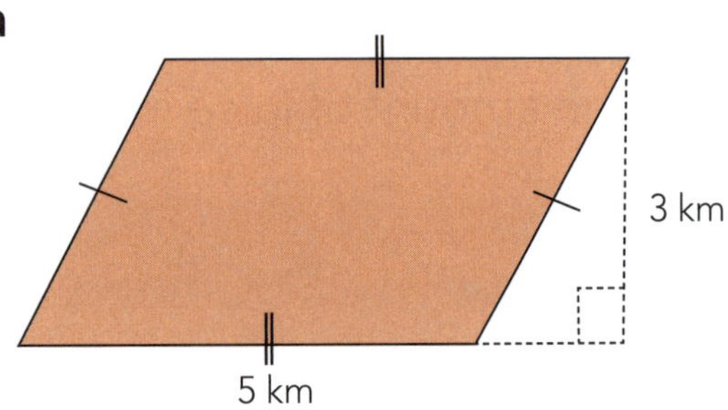

b

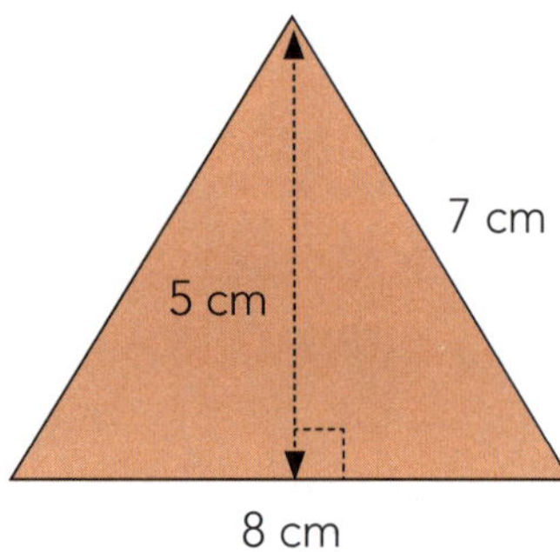

c

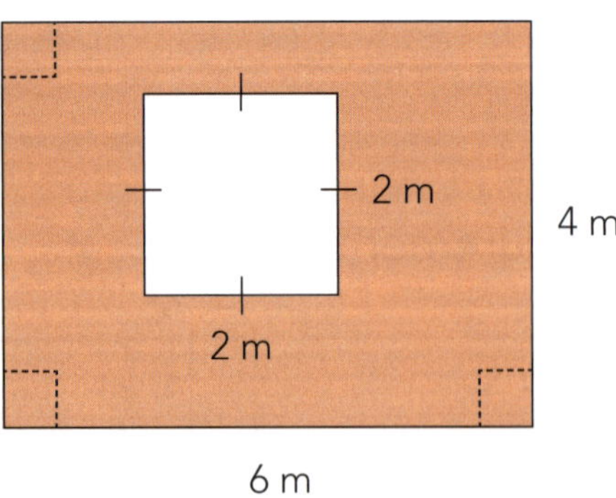

12 Calculate the volume of this cuboid.

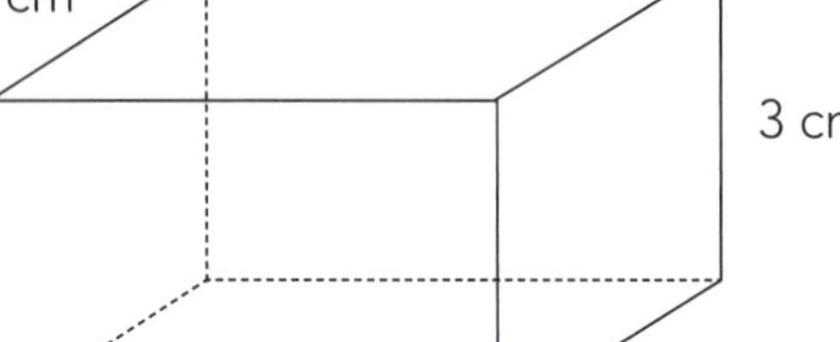

 ISBN: 9780170447171

Revision 2

1 Write the abbreviations for these units.

a kilometre ____________ b milligram ____________

c litre ____________ d teaspoon ____________

2 Write the meaning of these abbreviations.

a m ____________ b mL ____________

c kg ____________ d min ____________

3 Convert these measurements.

a 120 s = ________ min b 900 cm = ________ m

c 2000 mg = ________ g d 2 L = ________ mL

e 3 km = ________ m f 3 d = ________ h

g 4 m = ________ cm h 4 kg = ________ g

i 3 h = ________ min j 80 mm = ________ cm

4 Convert these times into digital time.

a Five past seven:

________ a.m.

b Quarter to ten:

________ p.m.

c a.m. = ________

d

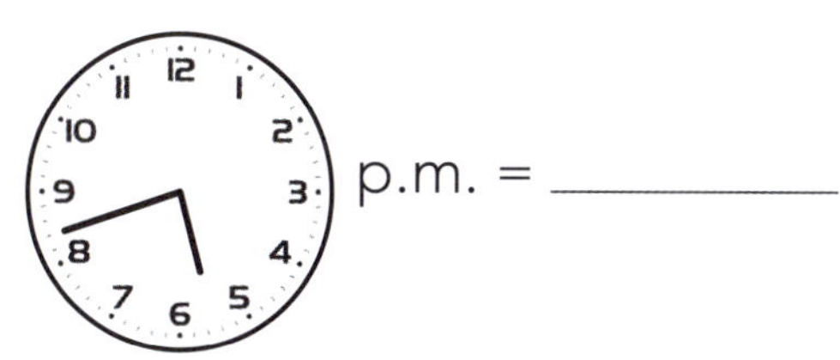

p.m. = ________

ISBN: 9780170447171

5 Convert these times to 12-hour times.

a 09:52 = ______________ b 18:24 = ______________

6 Convert these times to 24-hour times.

a 7.48 a.m. = ______________ b 5.31 p.m. = ______________

c Ten to five p.m. d Twenty past two p.m.

= ______________ = ______________

7 Circle or highlight the most likely unit of measurement for these items.

a The length of your tongue.

mL cm s kg

b The weight of a bumblebee.

L g mL cm

c The mass of a cake of soap.

tbsp g mm t

d The length of a school lesson.

years cm kg min

8 Write the measurements given by the pointers or scales.

A = __________ B = __________ C = __________

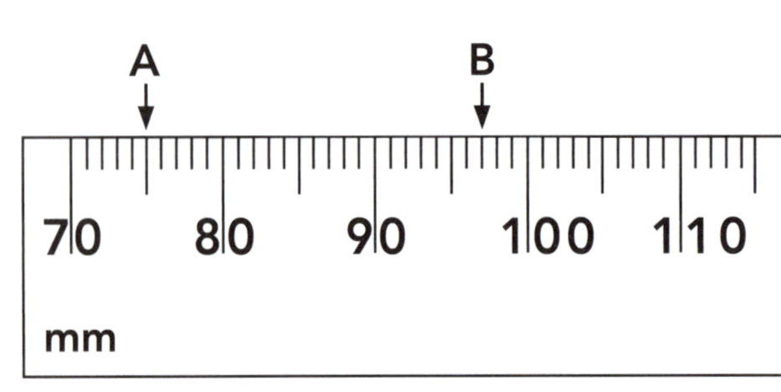

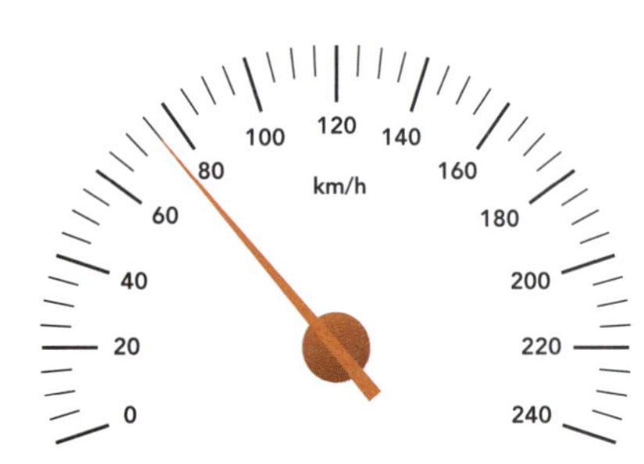

9 Colour the diagrams to show these measurements.

a 45 mL

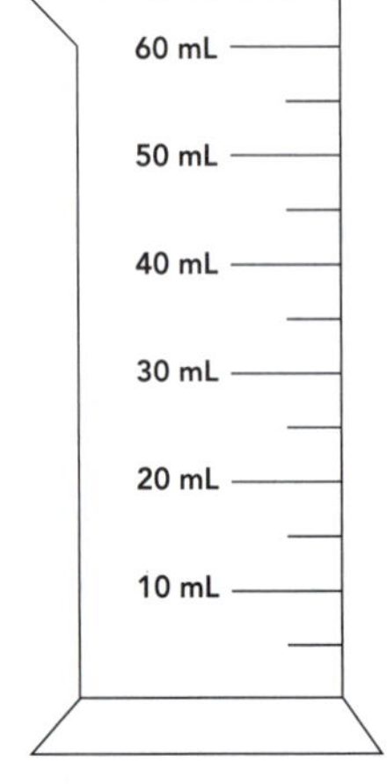

b 68°C

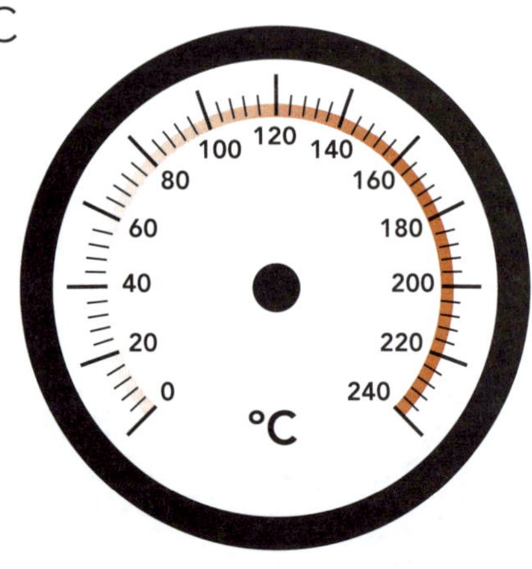

 ISBN: 9780170447171

10 Calculate the perimeters of these shapes.

a

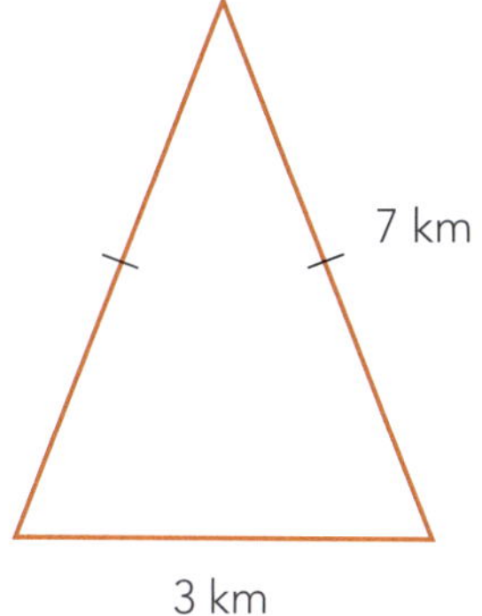

b

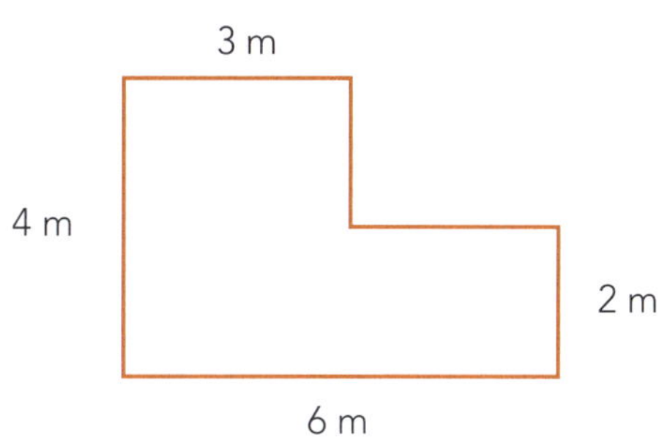

11 Calculate the shaded areas of these shapes.

a

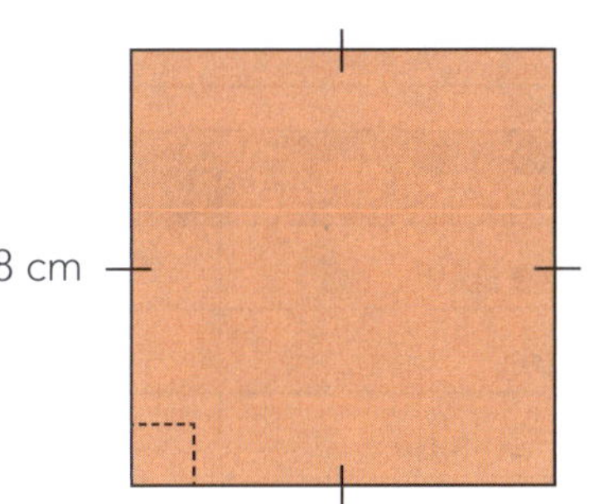

b

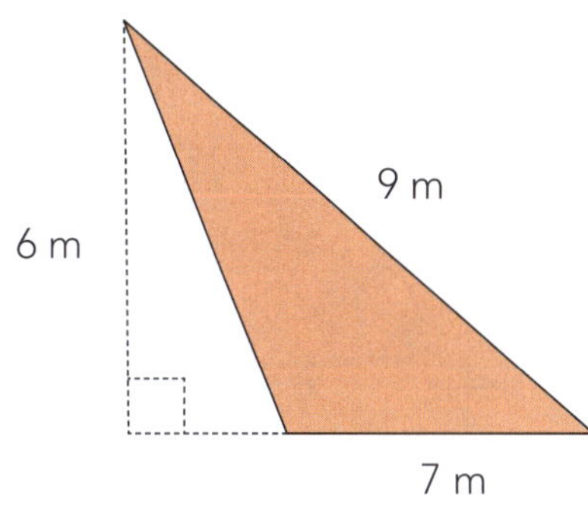

c

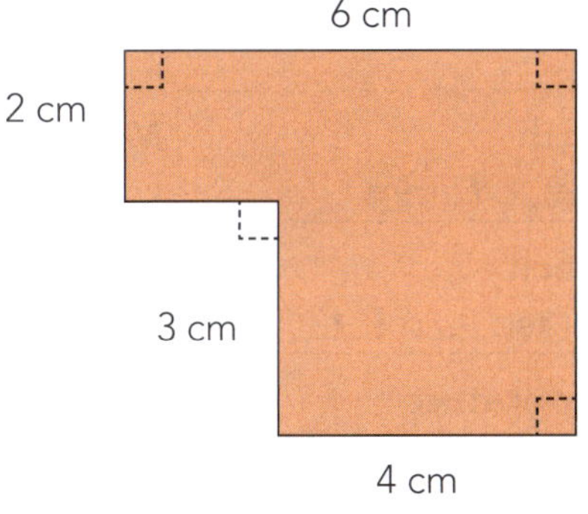

12 Calculate the volume of this cuboid.

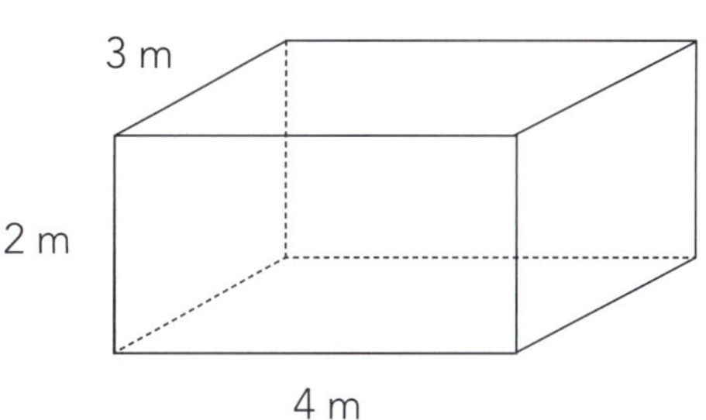

Answers

The language of measurement (pp. 6–7)

Length: short, long, distance
Time: early, late, day, week
Volume/Capacity: full, empty
Angle: steep, flat, decline, slope
Temperature: hot, cold, warm, heat, fever
Mass: heavy, light

Useful terms (p. 7)

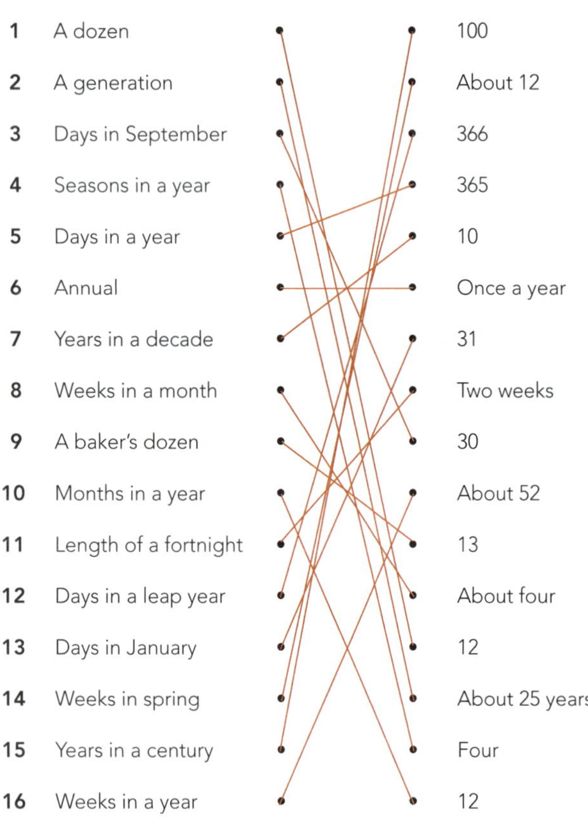

Measuring devices (p. 8)

Length: tape measure, ruler, pedometer, odometer
Mass: scales
Time: stopwatch, timer, clock
Capacity: cup, syringe, teaspoon, tablespoon, measuring cup
Angle: protractor, magnetic compass
Temperature: thermometer

1 Protracter
2 Odometer
3 Compass
4 Tape measure
5 Ruler
6 Pedometer

Units (pp. 9–24)

Abbreviations (shortened versions) for units (p. 9)

Unit of measurement	Shortened version
Kilogram	kg
Centimetre	cm
Metre	m
Minute	min
Litre	L
Hour	h
Milligram	mg
Teaspoon	tsp
Day	d

Unit of measurement	Shortened version
Kilometre	km
Millimetre	mm
Degree Celsius	°C
Second	s
Tablespoon	tbsp
Tonne	t
Millilitre	mL
Cup	c
Gram	g

Length km, m, cm, mm	**Mass** kg, g, mg, t
Capacity tbsp, tsp, L, mL, c	**Time** min, s, d, h
Temperature °C	

Time (pp. 10–11)

1 120 min
2 240 s
3 48 h
4 2 min
5 1440 min
6 1.5 h
7 5 min
8 72 h
9 10 h
10 240 min

ISBN: 9780170447171

11 200 min
12 150 h
13 2 min
14 6 h
15 300 h
16 2 h
17 97 h
18 1 d
19 1 d, 1450 min, 25 h, 93 600 s
20 minutes
21 seconds
22 days
23 hours
24 seconds
25 hours

Length (pp. 12–14)

1 2000 m
2 6 m
3 500 cm
4 0.3 cm
5 80 km
6 100 000 cm
7 70 mm
8 600 cm
9 5 km
10 1500 m
11 24 m
12 850 mm
13 110 mm
14 25 m
15 5 km
16 54 cm
17 301 cm
18 900 mm
19 100 cm, 10 000 mm, 100 m, 1 km
20 500 cm, 5500 mm, 55 m, 0.5 km
21 mm or cm
22 mm
23 mm or cm
24 km
25 mm or cm
26 m
27 mm
28 km
29 305 cm
30 6 m
31 21 cm
32 124 km
33 9 mm
34 1.4 cm
35 76 cm

Mass (pp. 15–17)

1 3000 mg
2 2000 g
3 4 g
4 5000 kg
5 80 000 mg
6 10 t
7 12 000 g
8 3000 kg
9 5 g
10 6.5 kg
11 15 000 mg
12 20 t
13 9001 mg
14 4 kg
15 30 g
16 20 000 kg
17 5 t
18 1 kg
19 10 000 mg, 10 kg, 100 000 g, 1 t
20 900 g, 9 000 000 mg, 99 kg, 0.1 t
21 t
22 kg
23 g
24 mg
25 g
26 g
27 kg
28 kg
29 450 kg
30 1.5 t
31 113 g
32 3.31 g
33 1 mg
34 1 kg
35 100 kg

Capacity (pp. 18–19)

1 1000 mL
2 4 L
3 65 L
4 2500 mL
5 9000 mL
6 6 L
7 11 L
8 1500 mL
9 24 000 mL
10 75 L
11 1 L, 1001mL, 1010 mL, 1100 mL, 10 L
12 1000 mL, 1050 mL, 1.5 L, 5 L, 5001 mL
13 1000 L
14 250 mL
15 5 mL
16 700 mL
17 26 L
18 8 L

Appropriate units (p. 20)

1 km
2 mL
3 g
4 min
5 cm
6 mL
7 t
8 cm
9 L
10 s
11 cm
12 kg

Estimating quantities (p. 21)

A

1 2518 m
2 72 km
3 15 mm
4 18 cm
5 30.5 m
6 1.5 m
7 1600 km
8 70 mm

B

1 550 kg
2 20 L
3 420 g
4 191 g
5 0.01 g
6 14.8 mL
7 5 kg
8 1 500 000 L
9 2.7 g
10 18 t

Conversion cross-number (pp. 22–23)

[1] 1	[2] 5	0		[3] 3	[4] 2	[5] 0		[6] 1	[7] .	[8] 7
[9] 3	0		[10] 8	0	0	.	0		[11] 1	2
[12] 0	.	5		[13] 0	.	8		[14] 4	5	0
[15] 1	3		[16] 6	.	0	0	[17] 0		[18] 1	0
0		[19] 9	.	0		[20] 0	.	[21] 3		0
	[22] 1	4	0				[23] 3	6	6	
[24] 7		[25] 7	2	[26] 0		[27] 1	6	0		[28] 9
[29] 5	[30] 2		[31] 0	.	[32] 5	0	0		[33] 3	1
[34] 6	.	0		[35] 3	6	5		[36] 2	2	4
[37] 0	4		[38] 4	8	.	0	0		[39] 9	8
[40] 1	0	0		[41] 1	4	4		[42] 7	.	0

ISBN: 9780170447171

Word questions (p. 24)

1	180 g	**2**	540 g
3	360 cm	**4**	7 km

5 7 minutes

6 1080 g or 1.080 kg in a 30-day month

7 **a** 2044 km in 365 days

b 1769.6 km in 316 days

Time (pp. 25–33)

Digital and analogue time (pp.25–28)

1	1.30	**2**	5.15
3	10.45	**4**	7.35
5	12.50 a.m.	**6**	6.20 p.m.
7	12.35 a.m.	**8**	10.10 p.m.
9	9.07 a.m.	**10**	4.42 p.m.
11	8.45 a.m.	**12**	4.05 a.m.
13	4.40 a.m.	**14**	11.20 p.m.
15	2.15 a.m.	**16**	1.30 p.m.
17	10.50 p.m.	**18**	12.00 p.m.
19	12.00 p.m.	**20**	12.00 a.m.

21 Half past eleven or eleven thirty

22 Quarter past seven or seven fifteen

23 Twenty-five to six or five thirty five

24 Ten to five or four fifty

25 Twenty past nine or nine twenty

26 Quarter to ten or nine forty five

27	10.15 p.m.	**28**	4.20 p.m.
29	9.42 a.m.	**30**	1.25 p.m.
31	2.05 a.m.	**32**	9.25 p.m.
33	9.50 p.m.	**34**	12.58 p.m.

Connect the dots (p. 28)

Digital time	Analogue time	Time with words
2.45		Twenty to three
4.15		Quarter to three
4.10		Ten to five
5.25		Half past four
4.50		Quarter past four
2.40		Ten past four
4.30		Twenty-five past five

24- and 12-hour time (pp. 29–32)

1	18:43	**2**	05:21
3	10.19 p.m.	**4**	21:56
5	5.38 p.m.	**6**	08:12
7	7.39 a.m.	**8**	8.42 p.m.
9	3.06 p.m.	**10**	2.17 a.m.
11	10.01 p.m.	**12**	5.23 p.m.
13	9.56 a.m.	**14**	2.45 p.m.
15	06:17	**16**	15:30
17	20:43	**18**	02:39
19	23:10	**20**	13:52
21	12:05	**22**	22:15
23	16:40	**24**	19:10
25	15:40	**26**	23:25
27	08:45	**28**	04:05
29	16:40	**30**	23:20
31	02:15	**32**	13:30
33	22:50	**34**	12:00
35	02:51	**36**	6.59 p.m.
37	8.23 p.m.	**38**	07:25
39	12:10	**40**	20:00

41 05:17, 7.05 a.m., 15:17, 17:03, 5.07 p.m.

42 6.16 a.m., 06:18, 16:20, 6.18 p.m., 18:20

		12-hour time	24-hour time
43	One minute past midday.	12:01 p.m.	12:01
44	Twenty-five minutes before midnight.	11:35 p.m.	23:35
45	Just before lunch at quarter to twelve.	11:45 a.m.	11:45
46	Five to one in the morning.	12:55 a.m.	00:55
47	One fifty-nine in the afternoon.	1:59 p.m.	13:59
48	Two minutes after midnight.	12.02 a.m.	00:02

Word questions (p. 33)

1	3.06 or 15.06	**2**	4.12 p.m.
3	11.50 a.m.	**4**	8.30
5	10.15 a.m.	**6**	36 minutes
7	Noon	**8**	4.06 p.m.

Reading tables (p. 34)

1 **a** 3 **b** 09:33

c 9 minutes **d** 09:15

2 **a** 19:35 **b** 25 minutes

c 19:02 **d** 19:30

 ISBN: 9780170447171

Scales (pp. 35–39)

Understanding scales (pp. 35–36)

1

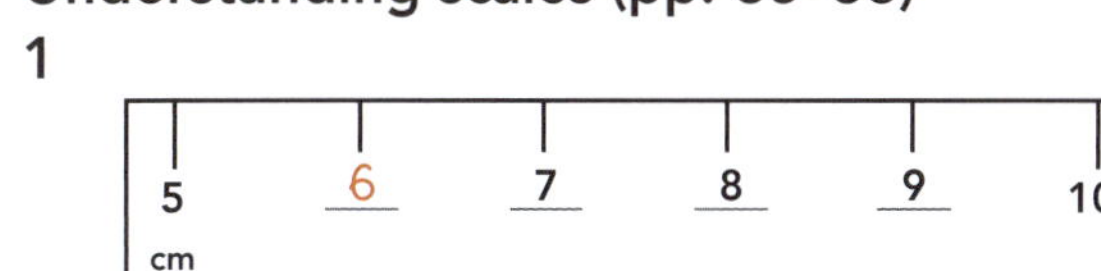

2

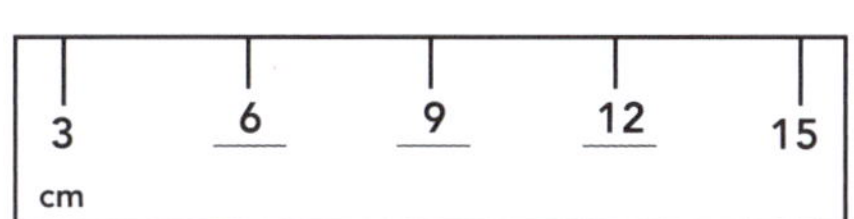

Size of gap = $\frac{\text{interval}}{\text{gaps}}$

= $\frac{15 - 3}{4}$

= 3 cm

3

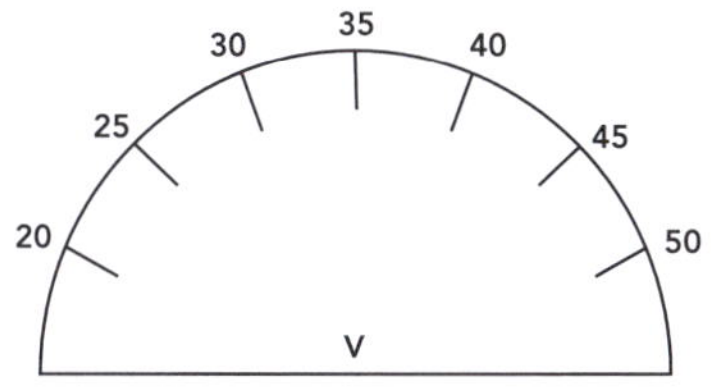

Size of gap = $\frac{\text{interval}}{\text{gaps}}$

= $\frac{40 - 20}{4}$

= 5 V

4

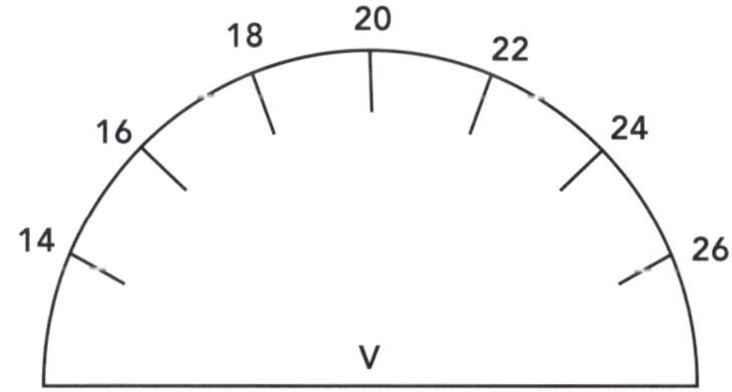

Size of gap = 2 V

5

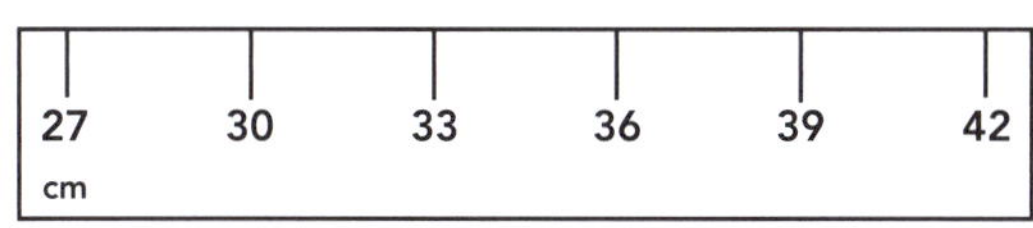

Size of gap = 3 cm

Reading scales (pp. 37–38)

1 A = 2.0 cm
B = 3.5 cm
C = 5.2 cm

2 35 mL
3 35°C
4 90 km/h
5 74 kg
6 D = 80 mm
E = 105 mm
F = 134 mm
7 12 V
8 43 V
9 45 km/h
10 115 km/h

Showing values on scales (p. 39)

1 2

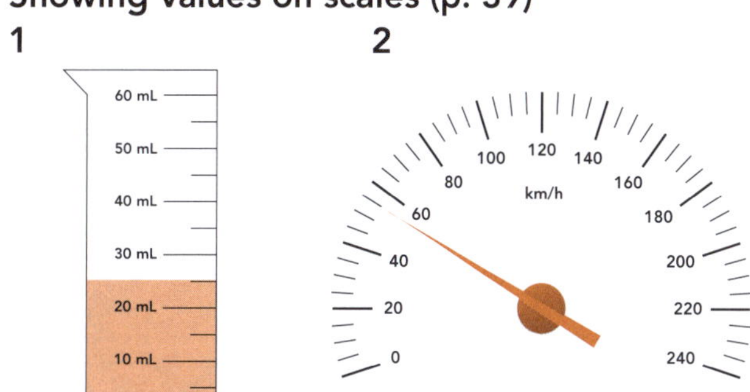

3

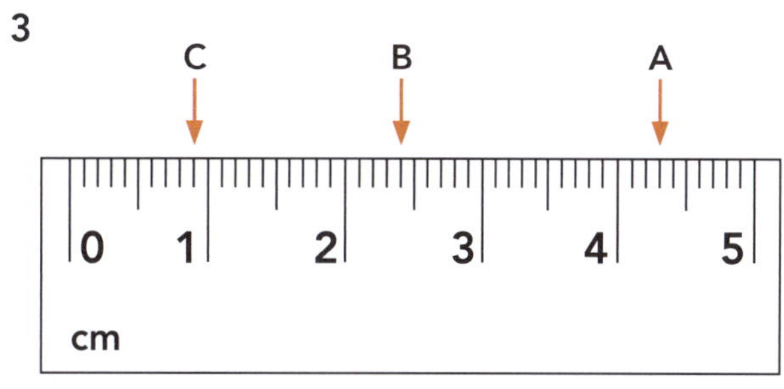

4 5

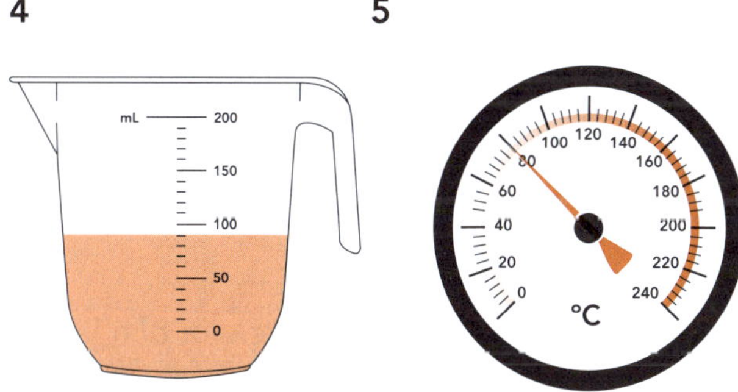

Perimeter (pp. 40–56)

Shapes on a grid (pp. 40–41)

1 A = 18 cm
B = 20 cm

2 C = 24 cm D = 22 cm
E = 20 cm

3 F = 24 cm
G = 36 cm

Shapes with linear sides (pp. 42–43)

1 18 m
2 120 mm
3 24 cm
4 20 m
5 19 km
6 14 m
7 140 mm
8 44 cm
9 18 m
10 14.5 km

Symbols on diagrams (pp. 44–45)
1 20 cm 2 55 mm
3 23 m 4 36 cm
5 4 km 6 36 cm
7 50 mm 8 22 m

Things to look out for (pp. 46–48)
1 36 cm 2 34 m
3 24 m 4 80 mm
5 16 km 6 10 000 m
7 14 km 8 280 mm
9 7 km 10 20 cm
11 35 cm 12 15 m

Working backwards (pp. 49–50)
1 5 m 2 7 mm
3 6 km 4 16 cm
5 1.2 km 6 4 cm

Compound shapes (p. 51)
1 26 cm 2 22 m
3 26 km 4 240 mm
5 20 m 6 24 m or 2400 cm

Compound shapes with missing measurements (pp. 52–53)
1 20 m
2 32 km 3 220 mm
4 22 m 5 26 cm
6 44 km 7 24 m or 2400 cm

Word questions (pp. 54–55)
1 8 m 2 150 mm
3 12 km 4 11 cm
5 15 mm 6 96 cm
7 9 m 8 800 cm or 8 m

Challenge 1 (p. 56)
1 120 cm 2 50 m

Area (pp. 57–76)

Shapes on a grid (pp. 57–58)
1 A = 15 cm^2
B = 10 cm^2
2 C = 16 cm^2
D = 12 cm^2
E = 19 cm^2
3 F = 38 cm^2
G = 27 cm^2

Rectangles on a grid (p. 59)
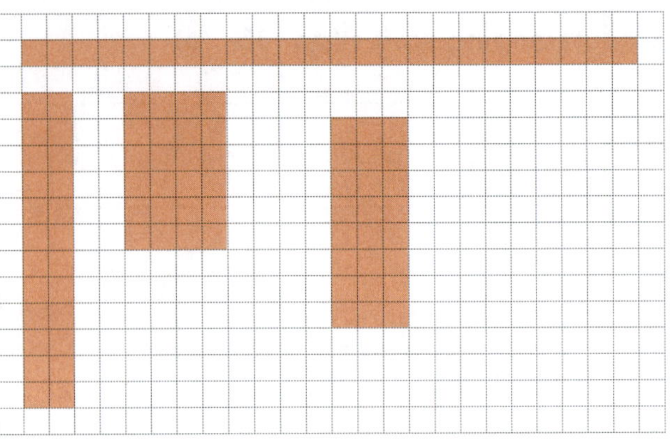

Rectangles using the formula (p. 60)
1 12 cm^2 2 14 cm^2

Quadrilaterals (pp. 61–64)
Square and rectangle (pp. 61–62)
1 21 m^2 2 25 cm^2
3 16 km^2 4 24 cm^2
5 24 mm^2 6 36 m^2
7 4 km^2 8 80 mm^2

Parallelogram and rhombus (pp. 63–64)
1 12 cm^2 2 60 mm^2
3 10 m^2 4 24 km^2
5 42 cm^2 6 4000 mm^2
7 12 m^2 8 140 cm^2

Triangles (pp. 65–66)
1 5 km^2 2 40 mm^2
3 21 cm^2 4 18 m^2
5 24 km^2 6 55 mm^2

Things to look out for (pp. 67–68)
1 12 m^2 2 24 m^2
3 20 cm^2 4 14 cm^2
5 1000 mm^2 6 2 km^2
7 12 m^2 8 3 m^2

Working backwards (pp. 69–70)
1 9 cm 2 5 m
3 5 km 4 6 cm
5 14 m 6 6 m

Compound shapes (pp. 71–72)
1 27 cm^2 2 104 m^2
3 32 cm^2 4 21 km^2
5 88 mm^2 6 90 m^2

ISBN: 9780170447171

Shapes with holes (pp. 73–74)

1 47 cm^2 2 5800 mm^2
3 38 km^2 4 27 m^2
5 74 cm^2 6 27 m^2
7 64.5 cm^2

Word questions (p. 75)

1 3.15 m^2 2 3 m^2
3 420 m^2 4 2700 cm^2
5 37.5 m^2 6 4 cm

Challenge 2 (p. 76)

1 41.5 cm^2 2 44 m^2

Volume (pp. 77–83)

Cuboids with cube blocks (pp. 77–78)

1 6 cm^3 2 8 cm^3
3 12 cm^3 4 9 cm^3
5 18 cm^3 6 8 cm^3
7 24 cm^3 8 48 cm^3

Cuboids using the formula (pp. 79–80)

1 56 cm^3 2 3000 mm^3
3 110 m^3 4 135 cm^3
5 720 mm^3 6 72 m^3
7 180 cm^3 8 216 cm^3

Things to look out for (p. 81)

1 1080 cm^3 2 168 m^3
3 198 cm^3 4 6 m^3

Working backwards (p. 82)

1 4 cm 2 3 m
3 7 cm

Mixing it up (p. 83)

1 96 m^3 2 5 cm
3 5 m 4 360 cm^3
5 120 m^3 6 7 m

Revision 1 (pp. 84–86)

1 a cm b s
c g d mL
2 a tablespoon b kilometre
c millimetre d litre
3 a 120 s b 9 cm
c 9000 mg d 5000 mL
e 300 cm f 240 min
g 4000 m h 3 g
i 2 d j 5 m
4 a 9.15 a.m. b 3.50 p.m.
c 2.35 a.m. d 8.54 p.m.
5 a 6.14 a.m. b 9.09 p.m.
6 a 09:51 b 15:15
c 20:30 d 21:55
7 a min b mm
c kg d mL
8 a A = 1.5 cm B = 3.1 cm C = 55 mL
9 a b

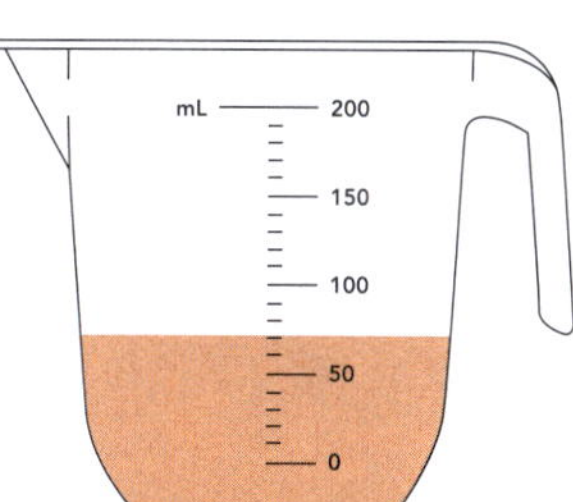

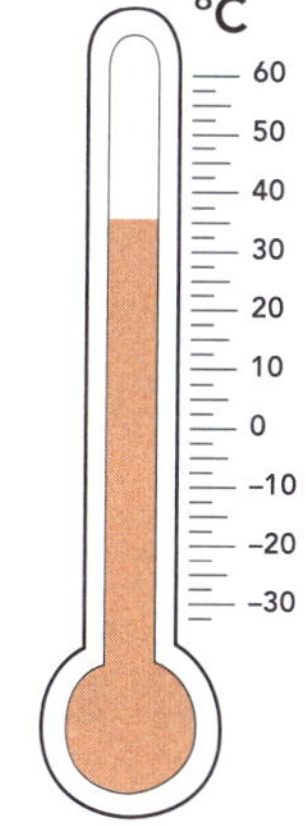

10 a 24 m b 22 mm
11 a 15 km^2 b 20 cm^2
c 20 m^2
12 72 cm^3

Revision 2 (pp. 87–89)

1 a km b mg
c L d tsp
2 a metre b millilitre
c kilogram d minute
3 a 2 min b 9 m
c 2 g d 2000 mL
e 3000 m f 72 h
g 400 cm h 4000 g
i 180 min j 8 cm
4 a 7.05 a.m. b 9.45 p.m.
c 9.24 a.m. d 5.42 p.m.
5 a 09.52 a.m. b 6.24 p.m.
6 a 07:48 b 17:31
c 16:50 d 14:20
7 a cm b g
c g d min
8 a A = 75 mm B = 97 mm C = 75 km/h

9 a

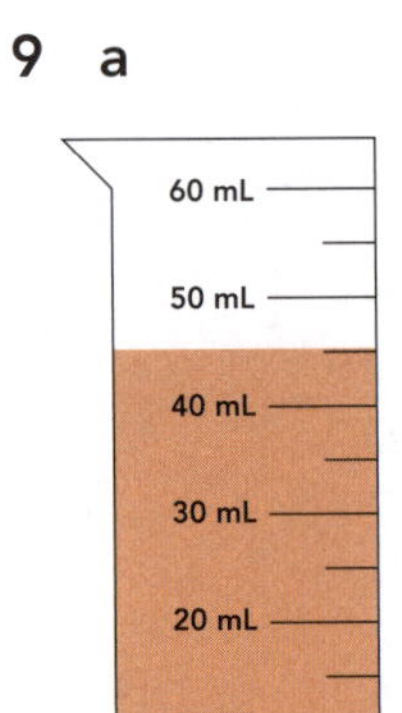

b

10 a 17 km **b** 20 m

11 a 64 cm^2 **b** 21 m^2

c 24 cm^2

12 24 m^3

 ISBN: 9780170447171